Successful Teaching in the Differentiated Classroom

Carolyn Coil

Pieces of Learning

CLC0335
© 2007 Pieces of Learning
ISBN 978-1-931334-48-8
www.piecesoflearning.com
Printed by McNaughton & Gunn, Inc
Saline MI U.S.A.
10/2013

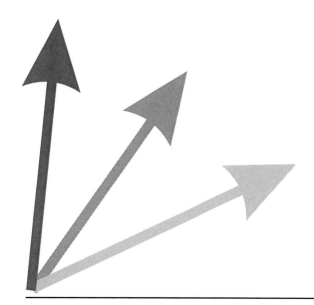

Acknowledgments

With thanks to all the teachers who have attended my workshops
during the past five years. Much of this book is a reflection of
what I have learned from you.

With special thanks for specific contributions to this book:

Kathy Wertz, Prairie Heights Middle School, La Grange, Indiana

Sharon Hack, Prairie Heights Middle School, La Grange, Indiana

Steve Bsharah, Delano High School, Delano, California

and to

Stan and Kathy Balsamo, Pieces of Learning, for their help in editing, layout, and publishing this book.

Dedication

With special love to my grandchildren
all of whom were born in the first decade of this new century.
May your teachers see your wonderful individual gifts and talents
and teach you accordingly!

and

To my parents, who were born in the early years of the last century.
As members of the 'Greatest Generation' you taught me well,
gave me continuous encouragement,
and led me to believe in unlimited possibilities for my life.

Table of Contents

How to Use This Book

'Differentiation' is one of the biggest buzzwords in education today. Everyone talks about it, teachers are told they should do it, conferences and staff development sessions focus on it, but often teachers do not really understand what it means and how to implement it in their classrooms.

This book identifies and explains a myriad of strategies and approaches to use to differentiate instruction, curriculum, and assessment. It also shows exactly how to use and how to proceed with each strategy so that teachers can put them into practice. It is a hands-on, practical, how-to-do-it resource and guide for the most essential differentiation strategies and techniques.

Each chapter targets a series of related strategies for differentiation. Each chapter discusses definitions, background information, and associated research/resources, but the majority of each chapter shows a how-to approach in the classroom. In this book are sample lesson plans, student activities, rubrics, student guidelines and checklists, planning forms for teachers, sample letters to parents, teacher assessment forms, and more.

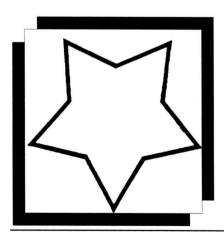

Because many of the pages are designed to be used directly either by students or by teachers, they are reproducible and ready to use. 'Reproducible' is clearly marked at the bottom of each of these pages. The CD-Rom that accompanies the book contains all of the Reproducible pages. Download them, print them out, and write your own lessons and ideas directly on the Microsoft WORD documents. Adapt or modify these forms, if needed, to make them even more useful.

At the end of each chapter is a page entitled '*To Summarize. . .*'. This page highlights and briefly reviews the most important ideas in the chapter. Read these pages carefully to make sure you understand the basics of what has been presented.

Throughout this book are '*Teacher Reflection Questions.*' They help teachers think through the concepts in depth and apply them to their own school or classroom situation. Use them either for individual thought and reflection or as a guide for teacher discussion in small groups, during workshops, or in professional learning communities.

It is my hope that after reading this book and using its many forms and guidelines, 'Differentiation' will no longer be a mystery or an impossible dream. Instead, I hope you will understand it as a rich and doable way to teach successfully.

Introduction

Differentiation

An Overview

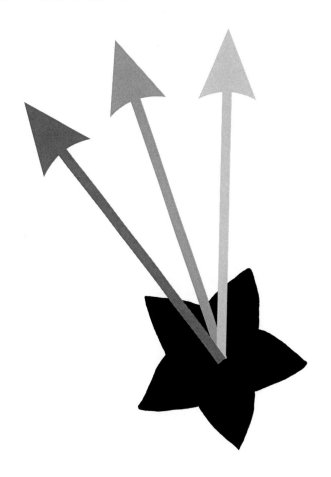

Differentiation: An Overview

Diversity is everywhere! Our foods, clothing styles, the languages we hear, and our religious and political beliefs all reflect this central reality in 21st century America. As classrooms are microcosms of the greater society, teachers, too, realize that diversity is everywhere.

Most teachers have discovered that teaching such diverse types of students doesn't work using the traditional 'one size fits all' approach. At one point in time, 'teaching to the middle' may have been an effective strategy. As students have become more diverse, however, teachers are increasingly seeking ways to diversify and differentiate their instruction.

A differentiated curriculum moves teachers away from the 'one size fits all' approach to curriculum that really fits no one! It encourages students to become more responsible for their own learning and to recognize and use their own strengths, thereby helping them become lifelong autonomous learners. Differentiation works best in a positive, encouraging classroom climate where students are led to take responsibility, accept challenges and learn as much as they can.

Brain research done in the past decade reveals much about how humans learn, and it provides yet another reason for differentiating curriculum. Learning occurs when the brain seeks connections to what it already knows. These connections form differently for each person because each person's experiences are different. They individualize our brains, and our learning experiences need to be, too.

Differentiation is particularly valuable with our diverse student population, because it is an approach to teaching that acknowledges differences in students and provides them with a variety of ways to learn. In examining learning options, we need to consider each student's interests, levels of readiness and ability, languages spoken at home, pace of learning, learning styles and modalities, strengths and weaknesses, and types of intelligences. On the other hand, we also need to bear in mind the state standards they require us to teach to all students. This is a big order for any teacher.

Simply stated, differentiated instruction allows each student to learn at the depth, complexity, and pace that is most beneficial to him or her. Differentiating curriculum and instruction is a rich and effective strategy to use when providing for the needs of all students, including those with special educational needs such as students with learning disabilities, gifted and talented students, and English language learners. They especially need differentiation when those students spend most or all of their time in regular classrooms.

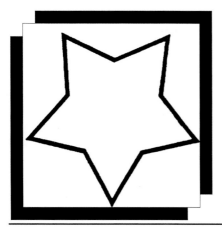

The Philosophy of Differentiation includes structuring classrooms so there are provisions for:

1. Different ways to take in, work with, and learn information
2. Differing amounts of time to complete work
3. Different approaches due to language acquisition and cultural differences
4. Different levels of thinking, readiness, and ability
5. Different assignments for students in the same classroom
6. Different means to assess what has been learned

Differentiation can be based on:

- Acceleration
- Enrichment
- Extensions
- Remediation

Acceleration allows the student to study the material at a faster pace and/or a higher grade level than would normally be the case. Collaborating with another teacher at a higher grade level is one way to find information and resources to use in acceleration. The most difficult aspect in using this approach is that it requires vertical planning between teachers at different grade levels, something that can be a challenge to schedule and implement.

Enrichment activities focus on studying areas or topics that are not included in the regular curriculum. These activities broaden students' knowledge and understanding on a wide range of subjects. Through exposure to enrichment activities, students may develop areas of interest or topics about which they previously knew little. Enrichment also allows students to explore current areas of interest in greater depth. This can lead to opportunities for investigations of real problems with links to the world outside of school.

Extensions use the regular curriculum as a starting point and allow students to delve into a subject more deeply or look at aspects of the subject or unit of study that may not otherwise be considered. Extensions work particularly well with students who already know the basics or who complete the regular assignments quickly and need additional challenges.

Remediation simply means that students have holes or gaps in their knowledge, skills, or learning that need to be patched before they can move on to more complex work. The assumption that all students begin the school year at the same starting point is a faulty one. Many times students lack the skills and knowledge to do the work their grade level requires. Finding out exactly what needs to be remediated for an individual student or for groups of students and then having a plan for accomplishing it is essential for student success in today's schools.

What is Differentiated in the Differentiated Classroom?

When we talk about the differentiated classroom, we are referring to the many aspects of the teaching and learning process that may be differentiated – that is, the things that may be approached in different ways for the different students in your classroom. Four of the most important are:

1. Content: This includes the ideas, skills, knowledge, and information being studied. Usually, content is structured by state standards, district curriculum guides, textbooks, and teacher-developed units of work. All students must learn the content, but they can learn it in different ways. Some students may learn it in more depth and complexity while others will learn the basics of content knowledge.

2. Process: This includes the various ways students interact with and think about the content. Often processes are defined by the different levels of Bloom's Taxonomy. For example, processes at the knowledge level might consist of memorizing, reciting, and defining while processes at the analysis level could involve comparing and contrasting, classifying, or subdividing.

3. Products/Performances: This includes the multitude of ways students can demonstrate what they understand, know, and can do as a result of their learning. Allowing for different products and performances is often the easiest way to begin differentiation in your classroom. Giving students a choice to develop one of several products to demonstrate their learning is motivational, takes learning styles into account, and creates variety in the classroom.

4. Learning Environment: This includes the physical classroom or learning space, how that space is used, available resources, and grouping patterns for students. A classroom where students always sit in rows in the same assigned seats is not an optimal environment for differentiation. A classroom with flexible grouping and seating arrangements, a variety of resources, and wall and shelf spaces to use for learning and displays of student work is a classroom that invites differentiation.

Throughout this book you will discover many differentiation strategies that cover these four areas. Pick the strategies and techniques that are the best fit for you. Because differentiation can be done in many ways, each differentiated classroom has a unique look and feel.

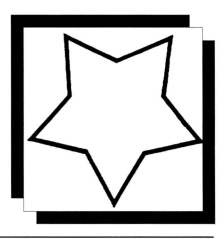

Four Important Concepts

There are four important concepts that help shape a differentiated classroom. Consider all four as you think about differentiation in your classroom or school. They are:

• Flexibility

The hallmark of a differentiated classroom is flexibility. Teachers skilled in differentiation must be flexible in their planning, flexible in how they structure groups, flexible in how they teach to various learning styles and modalities, and flexible in how fast or slow they proceed according to the individual learner. While flexibility is essential, it is also difficult because school systems prescribe the number of hours of instruction and the number of days in the school year or grading period. Some even stipulate the unit or pages of a textbook that must be covered within a given week.

Whatever the outside constraints, it is important to keep a flexible mind set. Try teaching in new ways. Give students multiple opportunities for learning. Be continuously creative in your teaching. This is all a part of flexibility.

• Planning

All good teaching requires planning. This is certainly true in a differentiated classroom where you must look beyond the grade-level standards and curriculum and focus on the learning needs of each student. Without careful planning, learning time can be wasted or the classroom can quickly degenerate into chaos.

On the other hand, no teacher has unlimited planning time. Most teachers are stretched with all the obligations and duties that are part of teaching in today's schools. Throughout this book, you will find practical, easy-to-use planning models and strategies that will make differentiation easier for you to implement. As you read, choose those you think will work best for you. Start with one or two and incorporate them into your normal daily or weekly planning. Eliminate strategies that don't work, and build on and enhance those that do. You will find that planning becomes easier and easier the more you differentiate on a regular basis.

• Resources

A differentiated curriculum requires many different resources. This may be quite a change if you have been using one textbook, with every child on the same page. Most schools already have many resources that are appropriate for differentiated classrooms. Rediscover the books, workbooks, manipulatives, computer software, and reference materials in your classroom, book room, or file cabinets. Ask yourself how you can use these materials to meet the needs of individuals or small groups of students.

Know what resources your school has. Often teachers have access to plenty of resources but need to spend time locating and organizing them and then choosing the ones that are appropriate to use. This is time well-spent and in the long run will save you planning time. Ask your school media specialist to help you find the resources you need for a differentiated unit or lesson. He or she is often your best human resource in locating other resources.

An excellent web site for locating many resources useful in differentiating curriculum and instruction is www.differentiatedresources.com. Log on to find resources in various categories, grade levels, and subject areas.

- **Choices**

Learning activities in a differentiated classroom often involve student choices. These choices include products and performances based on learning styles, learning modalities, Bloom's Taxonomy, or multiple intelligences. This does **NOT** mean giving students unstructured or unlimited choices. It **DOES** mean having a set of standards-based activities from which they can choose, at least some of the time.

In this book you will find a number of ways to design curriculum and learning activities that give students choices. Curriculum compacting, learning contracts, learning centers, independent study, tiered lessons, the ILP™ format, and Tic-Tac-Toe all are embedded with student choice. A word of caution – some students think that having choices means they can do nothing if they so choose. I believe that learning time is simply too valuable. For this reason, this is my rule about *choice*:

Carolyn's Basic Rule for a Differentiated Classroom

*The one choice you never have
is the choice to do nothing!*

Closing the Achievement Gap through Differentiated Instruction

Due to the No Child Left Behind Act (NCLB), many schools throughout the United States are reducing the amount of class time spent on any subjects other than reading and math. For some low-performing students and schools, all other subjects have been completely eliminated. Many educators in these schools are concerned about test scores and may feel they need to spend their time in repetition and drilling. Some claim that their schools are turning into test-prep factories.

When I discuss differentiation strategies with teachers in these schools, they often hesitate, wondering how this could be of help in their particular situations. They cite the test preparation strategies they are required to use, time constraints they feel when so many students are functioning below grade level, and the programmed curricula many of their schools use. At first glance, perhaps it is difficult to see how differentiated instruction could be of benefit in low-performing schools or how it could help close the achievement gap.

However, research done by Karin Chenoweth of the nonprofit Achievement Alliance tells quite a different story. She spent two years looking at schools that are making AYP and getting great results under very difficult conditions. The high-poverty schools in her project are from all over the United States. Most perform at the same level or higher as the wealthiest schools in their area. While each of these schools has an individual success story, there are commonalities among them. Their successes come from:

- Teaching using all of the senses, learning styles, and modalities
- Thematic units that combine math, science, literature, history, geography, writing, and the arts
- Integrating the arts into all aspects of the curriculum
- Hands-on projects with differentiated products and performances
- Pre-assessment, formative assessment, and data analysis that drives all aspects of instruction
- Individualized instruction and work depending upon how each student learns
- Flexible grouping based on skill levels and individual student needs

All of these are important elements of differentiated curriculum, instruction, and assessment. Looking at the successes of these schools, it would seem that differentiation is, indeed, a viable approach to closing the achievement gap.

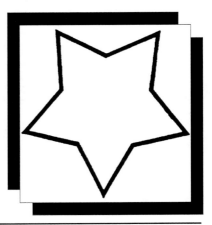

Two essential questions in differentiation are: What is "fair?" Does fair always mean "the same?"

Consider the conversation I overheard recently when I was a guest in a friend's home:

It was bedtime for three-year-old Hannah. Aaron, her five-year-old brother, was allowed to stay up an hour later. "OK, Hannah, it's time for bed," her dad said. "Why do I have to go to bed now?" she pouted. "Aaron isn't. It's not fair!"

Listening to this brief conversation, it struck me that even a three- year-old seems to have the impression that 'fair' most assuredly means 'the same.' When needs are different, however, fairness has quite a different interpretation. For example, suppose you had an appointment at the dentist's office to get your teeth cleaned.

Imagine this scenario:

"Good afternoon," the receptionist greets you. "We're preparing for your root canal." "Oh no," you quickly reply. "I'm just here to have my teeth cleaned!" "Well, I'm sorry but today is our root canal day. Everyone who comes in the office today gets a root canal. That's only fair!"

I suspect you would find a new dentist very quickly!

The idea of fairness is embedded deeply in our culture. Most people interpret being fair as doing the same thing in the same way for everyone. However, like in a good dentist office, in a differentiated classroom being fair doesn't always mean "the same." Fairness in school does not mean giving everyone the same assignment to complete within the same time period. Instead, it means looking at each student's needs and learning goals, and planning ways to meet those goals in a way that is most appropriate for that student.

My answer to the question 'What is fair?' is as follows:

> **'Fair' means that each student is doing the activity best suited for his or her learning.**
>
> **It does not mean that every student is doing the same learning activity.**

You, your students, their parents, and the administrators at your school must all believe in *this* concept of fairness in order for differentiation to be successful.

Because our students and their various learning needs are so different, the necessity for differentiation is obvious. All teachers would like to accommodate each child and meet the diverse needs they have. On a practical level, teachers look for workable strategies that can help them differentiate instruction in a variety of classroom settings.

There is no one magic strategy that works for every teacher in every school with every child. This book focuses on specific **practical** strategies that you can use to differentiate the curriculum, instruction, and assessments in your classroom. As you read, decide which strategies and techniques will work best in your classroom with your students. Start by using the Teacher Self- Assessment on the next two pages to assess yourself on your use of differentiation. Consider your strengths and weaknesses and areas in which you would like to grow.

Differentiating Curriculum: Teacher Self-Assessment

Assess yourself by responding yes, no, or sometimes (**Y, N,** or **S**) in each blank.

Do I give my students:

____ 1. Different ways to take in the information

____ 2. Different amounts of time to complete the work

____ 3. Different assignments depending on ability, readiness, comprehension level, learning preferences, or interests

____ 4. Different types of assessments to show what they have learned

For all students, do I:

____ 5. Use data to drive instruction, assessing readiness, skill levels, and content knowledge before beginning a unit of study and throughout the unit as students progress and learn

____ 6. Create a variety of activities and tasks for students to gather information, learn skills and concepts, and extend their knowledge

____ 7. Give students choices in some of their learning activities

____ 8. Focus on key concepts and standards for all learners, but allow them to explore these concepts and standards in different ways

For Gifted, High Ability or Advanced Students, do I:

____ 9. Make sure these students are challenged and have to 'stretch' their minds through higher-level thinking

____ 10. Focus on building leadership skills, social skills, and skills in delegation when they participate in mixed-ability groups

____ 11. Watch for stress, perfectionism, and fear of failure

____ 12. Use curriculum compacting, cluster grouping, independent study, and extension activities as appropriate

For Lower Ability Students or Students with Learning Difficulties, do I:

____ 13. Recognize that these students may have hidden talents and abilities

____ 14. Assess and emphasize their strengths as well as their weaknesses

____ 15. Motivate these students via relevant lessons and topics connected to their areas of interest

____ 16. Assess specific skills and knowledge that need remediation and have a variety of strategies to help students in these areas

For English Language Learners (ELL/ESL Students), do I:

____ 17. Give opportunities for these students to use English in a natural way while working on a project or activity

____ 18. Use lots of gestures, visuals, and graphic organizers when explaining skills and concepts

____ 19. Specifically pinpoint and teach the academic language these students need to know in order to complete an assignment or project

____ 20. Recognize cultural and experiential differences, and, when feasible, include these in units and examples

Based on this self-assessment:

My strengths in differentiation are:

Areas where I would like to grow and improve are:

To Summarize . . .
Introduction to Differentiation

➤ Differentiation acknowledges differences in students and provides an approach for working with them.

➤ Successful teachers consider differences in students' interests, pace of learning, readiness, abilities, and learning preferences (learning styles, learning modalities, and multiple intelligences).

➤ Approaches to differentiation include acceleration, enrichment, extensions, and remediation.

➤ Content, process, products, and the learning environment can all be differentiated according to the needs of individual students.

➤ Concepts that help shape a differentiated classroom include flexibility, planning, resources, and choices.

➤ Successful strategies used to differentiate instruction have been shown to be effective strategies for closing the achievement gap.

➤ In any classroom, 'fair' means that each student is doing the activity best suited to his or her learning needs. It does not mean that every student is doing the same activity.

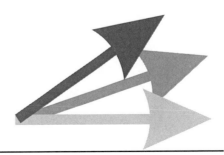

Flexible Grouping

Homogeneous
Heterogeneous
Individualized Instruction/Study
Whole group

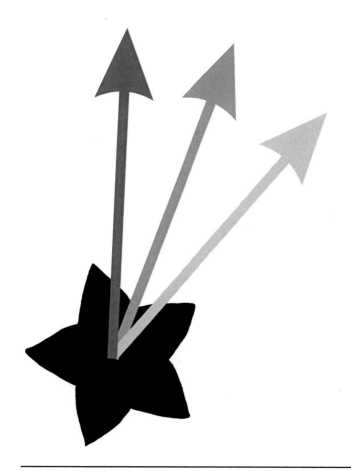

Flexible Grouping
A Basic Strategy in Differentiating

Flexible grouping is essential in the differentiated classroom. It is one of the basic teaching strategies for differentiating instruction. When teachers have a variety of learners in one classroom, the challenge is how to provide for all of their differing needs, interests, and abilities.

Individualizing for every student, in every learning area, every day is simply not possible or feasible. Therefore, one of the best and most practical ways to differentiate is through flexibly grouping students in a variety of ways, changing groupings as learning needs dictate. Even if you have a class designated as advanced, honors, or basic, you still have differing abilities and need to use the flexible grouping strategy.

When using this strategy, you should think of any instructional group as variable and temporary, not permanent. Flexible grouping means arranging for students to work together in a variety of ways and configurations depending on the classroom activity and desired learning outcomes.

One key to flexible grouping is to make sure students aren't in the same group for every classroom activity. When this happens, students can easily become categorized into the 'smart group,' the 'dumb kids,' the 'nerds,' etc. The danger in grouping without much flexibility is that students get into one group and stay there, even when the group is inappropriate for their needs.

An important question to ask as you plan learning activities for your students is:

> *What are the learning outcomes, and how can I best group my students in order to accomplish them?*

Basic guidelines for flexible grouping

- If prior skills and knowledge in the content area are not needed, use heterogeneous grouping or whole class instruction.

- If remedial or accelerated instruction is needed, use homogeneous grouping or individualized instruction.

- The logistics and classroom management for flexible grouping must be carefully planned. Well-functioning groups do not happen automatically! See pages 20-21 for specific details.

"Just moving their seats is <u>not</u> flexible grouping!"

Homogeneous / Ability / Cluster Grouping

- Groups students of similar ability, readiness, learning style, or interest.

- Usually based on some type of pre-assessment such as prior school performance, teacher observation, or standardized test scores.

- Use for remediation, acceleration, and enrichment.

- Can be used in multi-grade classes.

- Best to use when skills or prior knowledge are needed in order for the group to function well.

- Even in a class in which students are selected based on some set criteria (such as an 'honors' or 'remedial' class), you will still not have a homogeneous class. There will be differing ability levels in such a class, and flexible grouping will be needed.

Cluster Grouping for Gifted Students

A specific type of homogeneous grouping is called cluster grouping. In this grouping arrangement, a cluster of gifted and/or high ability students work together on a specific assignment or learning task.

Cluster grouping works best when groups of five to eight gifted or high ability students are clustered in one classroom with a teacher who has had training in methods to use to teach these students.

- As appropriate, a cluster of gifted and high ability students work together. Cluster grouping allows these students to learn from one another, do extensions of the regular classroom work, and work on suitably challenging tasks.
- Have daily blocks of time when students work together in the cluster group.

Note: In the same way, struggling students could be clustered for the remediation of specific skills.

Heterogeneous / Mixed Ability Grouping

- Groups students of differing abilities, levels, or interests.

- Improves socialization and understanding among different types of students.

- Facilitates the learning of common objectives and standards.

- Works best when reading level, math proficiency, or other specific skills are not involved.

- Use for cooperative leaning, discussion, role-playing, and affective curriculum.

- Good for group projects promoting creativity.

- Teaches skills in delegation, leadership, and sharing.

- Those who have learned the material can mentor those who haven't.

Note: Use this last strategy sparingly. You don't want a bright student to spend most of his time in school as the peer tutor for his classmates.

Potential Problems with Heterogeneous Grouping

While heterogeneous grouping has many benefits, it can also lead to problems. Often these problems occur when one student (usually a high ability student) does most of the work on the group project, but the entire group gets the same grade. This typically creates a great deal of resentment, but more importantly, if only one child is doing the work, the others are not learning.

One approach to deal with this problem is to make sure each student keeps a Learning Log or Work Record of his or her individual contributions to any group project (see page 27). A Group Self-Assessment (see page 28) is also helpful, as is the practice of appointing a Group Leader. The Leader's job is to make sure all group members are contributing to the group project or task (see page 29).

Individualized Instruction/Independent Study

These are discussed together because they use the same grouping pattern. For both individualized instruction and independent study, students work individually and generally complete the work on their own. However, each has unique components.

Individualized instruction *is a planned series of instructional activities or tasks that paces an individual student as he learns a portion of the curriculum.* Often each activity teaches another step in learning a specific skill or process. Individualized instruction is often used to teach reading, math, or foreign language. It can be done with pencil/paper learning packets, or cards, or through computer-assisted instruction. Many computer programs are designed to pre-assess frequently and then give students individual learning activities based on their level of readiness and expertise.

Independent study *allows the student more freedom in selecting a topic of study. It generally involves researching a topic in some depth and then demonstrating learning in some fashion.* Differentiated products and performances are a great way for students to show what they know when they have completed independent study.

Both:

- Facilitate the management of many achievement levels.

- Are self-paced learning at each student's performance level.

- Can be used for remedial, enrichment, or extension learning.

- Work well when students explore their own interest areas.

- Teach independent learning, organizational skills, time management, and the development of individual responsibility.

- Must be monitored and appropriately evaluated.

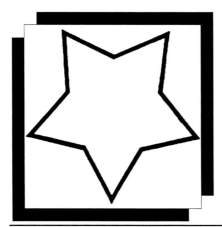

Whole Group Instruction

- Efficient and effective when presenting new content that all need to know.

- Works well with many types of AV presentations.

- Use for initial instruction and some enrichment activities.

- Needed when doing a highly motivational activity that should include all students.

- Use for guest speakers and also for your favorite lecture topics.

- Great for classroom celebrations.

Many teachers mistakenly believe they can never conduct a whole-group lesson if they truly differentiate their instruction. Nothing could be further from the truth! Teaching all of your students in a whole group setting is sometimes the best way to teach important points, give basic background information, build classroom camaraderie, etc.

The issue with whole group instruction is not that you should *never* use it. Instead, in a differentiated classroom you shouldn't always use it! Most teachers who successfully differentiate use all types of groupings in a balanced mix depending on their learning goals, students, learning environment, time constraints, and a host of other factors.

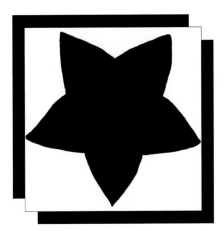

Guidelines for Managing Flexible Groups

1. Before grouping students for any activity, ask yourself: *"What is the learning outcome of this activity, and what is the best type of grouping to meet this learning outcome?"* Then group your students accordingly. See the **Flexible Group Planning Form** on page 25. Use this form as you plan various flexible groupings for a unit of work.

2. Use various types of assessment data to help you in forming groups.

3. Use some kind of record-keeper so you and your students will know at a glance who is in each group for a particular activity. Use color coding, numbers, clothespins, index cards, checklists, charts, or any other system that works for you.

4. Give explicit instructions about the task each group is going to do before the groups begin to work.

5. Teach students how to listen to one another as they work in a group. Distribute and go over **Guidelines for Listening When Working in a Group** on page 26.

6. Classroom rules and procedures for group work should be written, posted, and understood by all.

7. Model and practice procedures and routines for getting into groups so that movement becomes easy and automatic.

8. Common procedures and routines usually involve distributing, collecting and storing materials, moving chairs and/or desks for group work, getting help from the teacher, and monitoring/dealing with the noise level in the classroom.

9. Don't allow students to work in a group for too long a period. The length of time partly depends on the ages of your students and grade level of your class. It also depends on the maturity and attention spans of your students. Use your own good judgment as you would with any classroom activity.

10. Have a specific procedure for stopping group work and returning to a whole class setting. The more your students practice and do this, the less confusion and disruption there will be.

11. Each student should keep an individual learning log during group work. See a sample **Individual Learning Log for Group Work** form on page 27.

12. Have groups evaluate their own group process skills. One way to do this is by using a **Group Self-Assessment Checklist**. See page 28 for a checklist.

13. In some group situations, each student may have a specific role. In other cases, only a group leader needs to be designated. A **Group Leadership Checklist** can be found on page 29.

Flexible Grouping: Teacher Planning Form

When Should You Use Which Type of Flexible Grouping?

The answer to this question depends on:

- The structure of your school
- Your students' personal characteristics
- Ability levels of the students in your class
- Learning styles and modalities
- Student interests
- The learning outcome for each activity

Unit of work _____

List unit activities that will be done in each of these groups:

1. Homogeneous / Cluster / Ability Grouping

2. Heterogeneous / Mixed Ability Grouping

3. Individualized Work / Independent Study

4. Whole Class Instruction

5. Pairs or Partners

Student Guidelines for Listening When Working in a Group

1. Make sure only one group member is talking at a time.

2. Don't carry on a side conversation with someone else when you are meeting in your group.

3. Add your own ideas to what others have said. Connect your thinking to theirs.

4. Ask for clarification when you don't understand another person's ideas.

5. If you think you understood what someone else said, but you are not sure, repeat the main points, and ask if you are correct.

6. Concentrate on what other people in the group are saying. Don't daydream about something else such as what you will be doing after school.

7. Make sure someone is writing down important points or ideas.

8. Don't put down someone else's idea even if it seems to be a bad one. Instead, say, *"Let's think of other ways we could do it"* or *"Does anyone else have a different idea?"*

9. Wait for your turn to talk. Don't interrupt while someone else is talking.

10. Be aware of group members who talk all the time and don't give anyone else a chance to talk. In your group, discuss how you will function so that everyone has a chance to talk.

11. Monitor the noise level of your group and the class as a whole. If other groups in the room are so loud that you can't hear, tell the teacher.

12. If you have to leave the group for any reason, explain why you are leaving and when you will be back.

 © Pieces of Learning

Student Individual Learning Log for Group Work

Name _____

Date _____

Group tasks and accomplishments today:

What I did:

What the group did well together:

Ways to improve:

Date _____

Group tasks and accomplishments today:

What I did:

What the group did well together:

Ways to improve:

Working Together in a Cooperative Group

Group Self-Assessment Checklist

Rate your group according to the following scale:

1 = We didn't do this at all   2 = We need a lot of help in this
3 = We did well with this   4 = We were outstanding in this

Commitment to Purpose   Group Rating _____
Interest in task
Motivation to complete assignment
Followed directions

Work Process   Group Rating _____
Everyone participated
We didn't waste time
Ideas built on one another

Decision Making   Group Rating _____
Looked for solutions all could accept
Followed orderly process in making decisions
Decisions were not forced on some people

Communication   Group Rating _____
Listened to all suggestions
We stayed on task in discussions
Our talking did not disturb the class

Creativity   Group Rating _____
Considered new ways of doing things
Brainstormed ideas
No put downs for different thinking

Conflict   Group Rating _____
Established rules for dealing with conflict
Avoided personal attacks
Examined different points of view

Leadership   Group Rating _____
Group decided on leadership tasks and roles
Everyone took some responsibility
Group leader was fair to all

Group Members: _____   _____

_____   _____

Reproducible

Group Leadership Checklist for Student Leaders

As the leader of your group, you will be assessed on the following:

__ 1. You delegated jobs so that everyone participated in doing the group project or assignment.

___ 2. You helped the group use time wisely and have good time management skills.

___ 3. You helped the group plan the project, breaking the big task into smaller parts.

___ 4. You led the group in making decisions in an orderly way.

___ 5. You listened to suggestions from everyone.

___ 6. You made sure the group stayed on task during discussions.

___ 7. You led the group in brainstorming ideas, making sure all ideas and points of view were considered.

___ 8. You did not allow put-downs for different thinking.

___ 9. You helped the group establish rules for dealing with conflicts or differences of opinion.

___ 10. You treated everyone fairly.

To Summarize . . .
Flexible Grouping

➤ Groups in a differentiated classroom should be thought of as flexible and temporary, not permanent.

➤ Flexible groups are established based on the learning outcomes for a particular activity.

➤ The four basic types of grouping are homogeneous groups, heterogeneous groups, individualized work, and whole group instruction.

➤ Each type of grouping has advantages and disadvantages.

➤ Students need clear guidelines for moving into and working in groups. This is a process that takes practice.

➤ It is helpful to plan the types of grouping you will use during a unit of study. Use the Flexible Group Planning Form in this chapter to help guide your thinking.

➤ Students need a way to give the teacher both individual and group feedback when they work in groups. Choose the forms in this chapter that best meet your needs and the needs of your students.

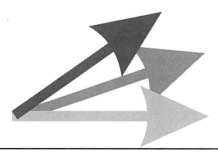

Curriculum

Compacting

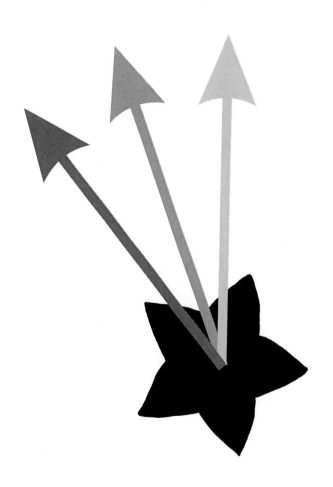

Curriculum Compacting: What Is It?

During my freshman orientation week in college, I was asked if I wanted to take a battery of tests. Since I was at freshman orientation to have fun, taking a test was not exactly at the top of my list! However, when I realized I could 'clep out' of some classes if I got a high enough score, I decided to take the tests after all. As a result, I got credit for several introductory courses that I didn't actually have to take.

My experience is not unusual. Many colleges give students credit for knowledge they already have. Curriculum compacting works in much the same way, but it is more focused on specific skills and knowledge rather than entire courses of work.

Curriculum compacting is a process originally developed by Dr. Joseph Renzulli and Linda Smith at the University of Connecticut. It provides a structured way to discover and record what each student knows before you teach a unit of study. It also serves as a planner to designate what your students' learning activities will be if they already know what is being taught.

The key to Curriculum Compacting is pre-assessment. This can be a pretest, graphic organizer, individual KWL chart, or any other method to find out what your students know. Those who already know the skill or skills you will be teaching document their mastery and 'test out' of the regular classroom work. This means they do not have to do class work or homework in the

skills they have mastered. Compacting students then work on a more challenging or higher-level alternate activity. I will discuss ideas and guidelines for alternate activities later in this chapter.

A list of grade-level skills and knowledge or state standards and benchmarks provide a good beginning point for identifying what could be compacted. Compacting works best with those skills that are very specific in nature – where it is obvious that a student knows about or knows how to do something or he doesn't. Therefore, many math skills work well with compacting as do spelling, grammar and mechanics, map skills, vocabulary, and identification of places, people, processes, etc.

Assessment for mastery is usually done at the beginning of a unit. On the other hand, at the middle or high school level some topics or skills may be completely new to all students. Within a few days, however, some students will have mastered the material while others need much more instruction, review, and practice. In this case, the pre-assessment might be done after initial instruction. In either case, students who already know the work do not have to continue doing regular classroom assignments.

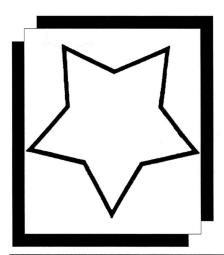

Curriculum Compactor Forms, Management, and Grading

Because students in the same classroom will be doing different work and different assignments, having a record-keeping form for curriculum compacting is most important. The Compactor Form lists the skills in one column, the score determining mastery (usually 85%-100%) in a second column, and the alternate activity in a third column.

Provide one form for each student. You can use the reproducible blank Compactor Form on page 36, or design one of your own. With the teacher's guidance or help, have each compacting student fill in the appropriate skills and knowledge he or she has mastered. In some cases, you may want to fill in the first and second column for the student. If you have a class with many high-ability students, you may want to design a generic Compactor Form with the targeted skills or knowledge already listed in the first column. Using this Form will make it easy for you and the compacting students to keep accurate records and appropriately document skill mastery.

Each student who is involved in curriculum compacting should have a folder or notebook in which to keep compacting work. Students often call this 'My Compactor.' In it should be all pretests and other pertinent data with dates, all Compactor Forms, and the work from alternate activities. Students are responsible for keeping track of their own compacting work. This is an excellent way to teach them organization and time management skills and a sense of responsibility. For some students, these lessons are more important than the academic learning in the alternate activities.

Knowing how to grade compacting students can be a challenge. In general, you do not want them to get a lower grade because they are doing more difficult work. Develop a procedure that works within your classroom grading system that will give compacting students credit for what they already know. Then include additional credit for the alternate activity. You can use the pretest score as a baseline, and go from there.

Make sure students understand that they do not have the choice of doing nothing! If a student chooses to do nothing, erase the pretest score, give no credit for it, and require the regular work. Students very quickly realize there are many benefits to doing the alternate activities and no benefit to doing nothing!

On the following pages are a Language Arts Compactor, a Math Compactor. ane a blank Compactor Form. Use these as models as you write your own.

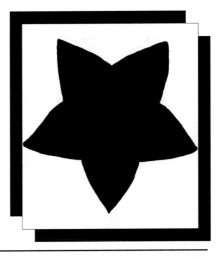

Curriculum Compactor for Language Arts

Standards or Benchmark, Content or Skill Area	Documenting Mastery	Alternate Activities
• Uses common rules of spelling and corrects words using dictionaries and other resources.	95% accuracy in spelling on written assignments	Create your own Challenge Spelling List with words you do not know how to spell. Use it to do any of the following: • Make a crossword puzzle. • Write a short story. • Develop an illustrated dictionary. • Create a song or poem. • Design word art. • Create a greeting card message.
• Demonstrates the ability to read orally with speed, accuracy, and expression.	90% accuracy on Fluency assessment.	• Create a reader's theater script based on a book you have read. Read aloud to the class. Choose additional readers if needed. • Go to another grade level for partner reading with another student.
• Identifies and infers main idea and supporting details.	90% accuracy on pretest	Select a book of your choice. Do one or more of the following: • Create a PowerPoint presentation detailing the main idea of the book. • Interpret the main idea through creative movement or dance. Perform for the class.
• Identifies and understands the uses of adjectives	Completes teacher-made pretest on identification of adjectives - 95%.	• Create a descriptive "Wanted" poster for the character in the weekly story. • Write a short story using adjectives. • Create a cartoon about being an "adjective." • Make a game board using adjectives as the theme.

 © Pieces of Learning

Curriculum Compactor for Math

Standards or Benchmark Content or Skill Area	Documenting Mastery	Alternate Activities
• Identifies fractional parts of a whole and as a part of a group.	90% accuracy on fractions pretest.	• Use website www.mhschool.com to generate games and other activities related to fractions. • Make a Fraction Wall using a different color for each fraction featured on the wall. Include pictures or other ways of illustrating fractions. • Create your own fraction code. • Write four math story problems related to fractions. Give them to a friend to solve.
• Knows multiplication and division facts up to 9x9.	85% accuracy on oral assessment.	• Make a collage showing how multiplication and division are used in everyday life. • Write a story entitled "The Land with No Multiplication or Division." Explain what would happen if people couldn't ever multiply or divide.
• Solves one and two-step word problems involving multiplication and division.	90% accuracy on pretest.	• Research the relationships between multiplication, division, and fractions. Make a chart or other graphic organizer to show what you learn. • Demonstrate how multiplication and division work through creative movement or dance. Perform for the class. • Develop a card game that involves multiplication or division. Play it with a classmate.

CURRICULUM COMPACTOR FORM

Student's Name _____

Skill, Knowledge, Benchmark or Standard	Documentation of Mastery	Student Choice Alternate Activities

© Pieces of Learning

Alternate Activities

I was explaining curriculum compacting to a group of students who were particularly skilled in math. After I had explained how compacting works, one boy questioned, "Why would I want to compact out of my work in math which I love, if I have to spend more time working on writing which I hate?"

His remark focuses on a particularly valuable lesson for teachers who are thinking about implementing curriculum compacting. Unless the student specifically requests it, do not use the time a student 'buys' from a strength area to remediate a learning weakness. Remediating a weakness may make good sense to the teacher, but it is not a motivator for most students!

You may want to give compacting students a choice of several alternate learning activities. Make sure these activities require higher-level thinking and are challenging to the students yet can be done independently.

Alternate activities are usually extensions, enrichment or acceleration of the same subject area from which the student 'bought' the time. Sometimes, however, they may be activities from different learning areas, from thematic units, or an independent study based on the student's individual passion or interest area.

Teachers are sometimes concerned that using curriculum compacting involves much more planning and work. They seem unsure of where to find appropriate alternate activities. However, if you organize compacting well, it should take only a minimum of extra planning time. Consider these sources for easily available alternate activities:

➢ Look in the Teacher's Edition of your textbook. Every unit generally comes with many suggestions for extension or enrichment activities. You may have looked at these and concluded you don't have time to do them with your class. Curriculum compacting actually compacts time. So your compacting students may have time to do some of these activities. Choose those that can be done independently with little direction from the teacher. Type two or three activities on an index card or piece of paper and give a choice to your compacting students.

➢ Look at the supplemental materials that come with your textbook. Most textbook companies ship a host of other materials along with the textbooks. Many teachers never use them because of a lack of time. Yours may still be packed away in a box somewhere! Look through them to see what may be appropriate.

➢ Use supplemental books that target higher-level thinking. You can often find these in the exhibit area of conferences, in catalogs that are sent to your school or home, or in teacher bookstores. Many of these books have alternate activities ready to use! *Pieces of Learning* has many such books. Favorites to use with compacting students include:

Math Rules	*Math in Fables and Myths*	*Word Play*
Think Hard	*Researching Adventures*	*Think Harder*

➢ Use supplemental books that give students a new activity for each day of the year. This helps compacting students know exactly which activity they will work on each day without specific directions from you. Examples from Pieces of Learning include:

Creativity Calendar   *Extra Credit*

➢ Use old textbooks or materials from your file cabinet or book room. Many of these contain wonderful activities for students. In fact, you still have them because they are too good to throw out, and you know you will use them 'some day.' 'Some day' has arrived! Pick out appropriate activities for your compacting students, or let them choose those they want to do.

Choosing appropriate alternate activities can be the teacher's job, but it can also be left to the student. See ideas and guidelines on the next page.

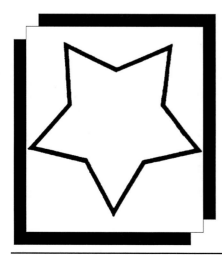

Giving Compacting Students Choices

Differentiation often involves giving students choices in the learning activities they will do. Choosing alternate activities for curriculum compacting is one way such choices can be given. Most students need guidance in making appropriate choices. Below are guidelines to share with your students.

Guidelines for Compacting Students

Because learning time is so valuable, the most important thing to remember is:

The one choice you never have is the choice to do nothing!

When you are compacting, your behavior and work habits are important. Therefore, you should never choose to:

- ➢ waste learning time
- ➢ goof off
- ➢ sleep instead of work
- ➢ disrupt the class

When choosing a learning activity, follow these guidelines:

1. The activity will help you learn something new or will extend your learning about a topic or idea.

2. You can do the activity independently without the teacher's help.

3. You have the materials you need to do the activity.

4. You have enough classroom space to do the activity.

5. You will not disrupt the class by doing this activity.

6. The activity is interesting to you.

Teacher Reflection Activity

With at least one colleague, discuss which skills and knowledge would be easiest to compact in your grade or subject. Use the first column in the form below to make a list of these; then brainstorm a list of alternate activities for your students.

Skills/Knowledge to Compact

Ideas for Alternate Activities

Reproducible

Parent Information and Involvement with Compacting

It is important to keep the parents informed when their child is involved in curriculum compacting. They need to understand why their child is doing something different from the rest of the class, why their work is more difficult, and how the grading will be handled. A sample letter is below.

Dear Parents,

During the next two weeks, we will be studying _____ in _____ class. Your child, _____, scored _____ on the unit pretest and has already mastered the unit skills and concepts. Because of this, he/she will not be required to do the regular class work for this unit but instead will be working on a choice of alternate activities. This is known as Curriculum Compacting, a well-known teaching strategy developed by Dr. Joseph Renzulli at the University of Connecticut.

Your child's grade will be based on the score he/she received on the pretest plus additional points for the alternate activities. Because these activities are more difficult than regular classroom work, I will be looking for effort, creative and critical thinking, independent work habits, and persistence in working through a difficult task. The goal is to extend and challenge your child beyond grade level work.

Thank you for your support. Feel free to call me if you have any questions or concerns. Please sign and return this letter to let me know you have received this information.

Yours,

_____ (Teacher's name)

_____ (Parent signature)

Variations on Compacting

Compacting is generally used when most of the students in a class need to learn and practice grade-level work, and a few students have already mastered it. Sometimes, however, classes end up having other configurations and needs. In these situations, you can still use the basic idea of compacting but with some slight variations as to how you will implement it. In the situations described below, you will see how you can use it in many different ways.

'Reverse' Compacting

If you have a class in which <u>most</u> of the students have mastered the skills, information, or learning objectives before you teach them, but a few have not, you may want to try "Reverse Compacting." In this situation, the teacher designs a Compactor Form listing the skills to be mastered. Alternate activities are the activities students will complete as they work toward mastery, each at their own pace.

In this circumstance, the teacher works with the majority of the students on extensions of the grade-level standards while checking with the reverse compacting students to look at their daily progress. If a paraprofessional or inclusion teacher is available, they can work more closely with the reverse compacting students.

This gives struggling students an opportunity to work using a Compactor, and it also helps them grow as independent learners. If there are several alternate activities to choose from as they master the skills, this gives them some control over their own learning.

'Half and Half' Compacting:
Half of the students have reached mastery and half have not

If you have a class fairly evenly divided between students who have reached mastery and ones who have not, you may want to give each group half of the instructional time and half of the 'compacting time.' In other words, each group will have some instruction directly from you, and each will have time to work on an appropriate alternate activity.

Compacting and Flexible Grouping within an Entire Grade Level

Sometimes teachers at an entire grade level within a school will pretest all of their students on a given set of skills or unit of work. Based on this pre-assessment, the students are then divided into classroom groups for instruction on that unit of work. Each of the grade-level teachers instructs one of these groups of students. For example, if there are three fifth grade teachers, each would take one-third of the students. The groups might be categorized as follows:

➤ **Extension Class** – For students who demonstrate mastery of unit concepts and skills
➤ **Concept Mastery Class** – For students who demonstrate strength in a majority of skills with a general understanding of unit concepts
➤ **Skill Development Class** – For students who demonstrate weakness in a majority of unit skills and concepts

This strategy is most often used in math. When it is done for an entire grade level, it is important to pre-assess students before beginning each unit of study. In addition, for each unit of study teachers should rotate so that over time all of the grade-level teachers will teach each of the classes.

Parent involvement and understanding of this instructional arrangement is essential. A sample letter to parents is below.

Sample Parent Letter for Compacting/Flexible Grouping for an entire grade level

Dear Parents,

This year the _____ grade teachers will use Curriculum Compacting as a tool to differentiate math instruction. It is designed to streamline grade-level curriculum and targets areas of content each student already knows as well as areas on which each needs to focus. Compacting is a three-step process:

➢ Assessing what each student already knows
➢ Planning what each student needs to learn
➢ Giving each student meaningful activities that will help to teach, extend, and enrich their understanding

Before we begin each math unit, each home room teacher will administer a pretest to each student. The results of this test will determine the most appropriate class placement for each student during that unit of study. Classes are as follows:

➢ Extension Class – For students who demonstrate mastery of unit concepts and skills
➢ Concept Mastery Class – For students who demonstrate strength in a majority of skills with a general understanding of unit concepts
➢ Skill Development Class – For students who demonstrate weakness in a majority of unit skills and concepts

Please note that your child's home room teacher may or may not teach your child math for each unit. Students will be placed in the class that best defines their levels of understanding and skill. Each teacher will take turns teaching the Extension, Concept Mastery, and Skill Development classes. Students will be grouped for each unit based on pre-assessment and prior knowledge. Groups will be flexible and will no doubt change throughout the year. At the beginning of each unit of study, you will be notified as to which class your child is in and who his/her teacher is for the unit.

Research suggests the benefits of compacting are many. It addresses the needs of each individual learner, encourages independence in learning, and increases motivation to learn. We are excited to have the opportunity to work with your child using this instructional strategy. If you have any questions, feel free to contact us.

Sincerely,

Using the Compactor to Record Mastery of Specific Skills within a Unit of Work

Sometimes a unit of work will contain a number of specific skills. It is possible that a student may have mastered some of these skills but not all of them. In this case, you can design a pretest that targets each of the skill areas separately. Tell students to skip any of the pretest items they don't know how to do. Remind them to do their best, and assure them that no grade will be given on the pretest.

Each student's pretest is marked for accuracy and a Student Evaluation Form is filled out. From this form, the student can readily see which skill areas he or she has mastered. 'Yes' is checked if the skill has been mastered prior to instruction and 'No' is checked if it has not.

When a particular skill is taught on a given day, students check their Student Evaluation Forms. Students who have 'Yes' on a particular skill have "compacted out" of listening to the instruction for that day. These students choose an alternate activity to work on while the instruction is taking place. Depending on the skill, the teacher may just be instructing a few students while the rest work independently or may be instructing most of the class while one or two work on alternate activities.

Instruction continues in this manner for each of the skills throughout the unit of study. At the end of the unit, all students take the final test which is formatted exactly like the pretest. In fact, the same test could be used as both the pre and post test. Again the Student Evaluation Form is marked. The goal is to have all skill areas marked 'Yes' at the end of the unit. With this method, students can easily see their improvement and can celebrate that they have learned so much.

This also serves as a good accountability document for the teacher and is helpful to use during Parent/Teacher conferences. Furthermore, having post test results allows the teacher to make sure all students have truly mastered the needed skills.

On the next few pages you will find:

➢ Sample Student Evaluation Form

➢ Sample Pretest and/or Post Test

➢ Blank Student Evaluation Form

➢ Alternative Activities Procedures

➢ Alternate Activities Student Feedback Form

➢ Sample Parent Letter

Student Evaluation Form for Curriculum Compacting

Dividing Whole Numbers and Decimals

Unit 4
Concept: Separation

Name_____ Period _____

Date of Pretest _____ Date of Posttest _____

			Pretest		Posttest	
Standards	**Objective/Benchmark**	**Items**	**No**	**Yes**	**No**	**Yes**
4.2.4	4-1 Review the meaning of division	1,2,3,4,5				
4.3.5	4-2 Explore pattern to divide	6,7,8,9,10				
5.2.6	4-3 Estimate using compatible numbers	11,12,13,14, 15				
5.2.1	4-4 Divide by a 1-digit divisor	16,17,18,19, 20				
5.6.2	4-5 Find the mean	21				
5.7.1	4-6 Solve problems by interpreting remainders	22				
5.3.1	4-7 Explore products and quotients	23,24,25,26, 27				
5.1.6	4-8 Find the factors of a number	28.29,30,31, 32				
5.1.6	4-9 Explore prime and composite numbers	33,34,35,36, 37				
5.7.3 5.7.9	4-10 Solve problems by working backwards	38				

Sample Pretest/Post Test

Dividing Whole Numbers and Decimals

Name _____Period _____ Date _____

4.2.4 4-1   Review the meaning of division.
Fill in the blank with each quotient.

1. $35 \div 5 =$ _____   2. $18 \div 3 =$ _____   3. $56 \div 7 =$ _____   4. $49 \div 7 =$ _____   5. $32 \div 4 =$ _____

4.3.5 4-2   Explore patterns to divide.
Find each quotient. Use mental math.

6. $2,100 \div 7 =$ _____   7. $540 \div 9 =$ _____   8. $900 \div 3 =$ _____   9. $25,000 \div 5 =$ _____   10. $160 \div 2 =$ _____

5.2.6 4-3   Estimate using compatible numbers.
Estimate each quotient using compatible numbers.

11. $144 \div 7 =$ _____   12. $734 \div 9 =$ _____   13. $312 \div 5 =$ _____   14. $189 \div 2 =$ _____   15. $467 \div 5 =$ _____

5.2.1. 4-4   Divide by a 1-digit divisor.
Divide. Find the quotients. Show your work.

16. $249 \div 3$ 17. $\$7.24 \div 4$ 18. $513 \div 5$ 19. $919 \div 9$ 20. $785 \div 6$

5.6.2 4-5   Find the mean.
Read the following and answer the question. Show your work.

21. Mrs. Smith's class did a survey to find out how much students receive each week for their allowance. Use the results of the survey below to answer the question.

$3.00 $6.00 $4.50 $4.00 $5.75 $4.50 $5.00 $6.05

What is the mean allowance for Mrs. Smith's class? _____

Sample Pretest/Post Test (continued)

Dividing Whole numbers and Decimals

5.1.6 4-8   Find the factors of a number.
Find **all** the factors for each number.

28. 16 _____   29. 12 _____   30. 49 _____

31. 22 _____   32. 30 _____

5.1.6 4-9   Explore prime and composite numbers.
Label each number as either prime or composite. Use a "P" or "C."

33. 9 _____   34. 23 _____   35. 27 _____   36. 39 _____   37. 11 _____

5.7.2. 4-10. Solve problems by working backwards.
Solve. Use the 5-step plan and the working backwards strategy.

38. Carlos bought a fish tank and some fish. When the fish were doing well, he doubled the number of original fish by buying more. then 6 of the fish died. Carlos corrected the chemicals in the tank. He bought 4 new fish. Carlos now has 24 fish in his tank. How many fish did Carlos originally buy?

Student Evaluation Form for Curriculum Compacting

Name_____ Period _____

Date of Pretest _____ Date of Posttest _____

Title of Unit

Concept

			Pretest		Posttest	
Standards	**Objective/Benchmark**	**Items**	**No**	**Yes**	**No**	**Yes**

     © Pieces of Learning

Directions for Doing Alternate Activities

1. Add your name to the Alternate Activities Sign-in sheet.

2. Select the alternate activity of your choice from the list.

3. Read and follow the directions completely. Finish one activity before moving on to another. Take pride in the work you do. Your "work" is a "mirror of you."

4. Be on your best behavior when working on alternate activities. Your voice should be no louder than a whisper if you need to talk to someone.

5. Monitor your own time as you work on alternate activities. Allow approximately 5-10 minutes at the end of the class to clean up, compete the Alternate Activities Student Feedback Form, and turn in all work using the alternate Activities Box.

Keep in mind:

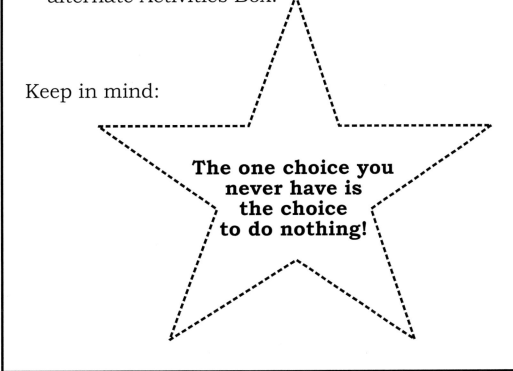

The one choice you never have is the choice to do nothing!

Alternate Activities Student Feedback Form

Name _____

For an alternate activity, today I chose . . .

_____

_____

This activity helped me to practice the skill . . .

_____

_____

_____

I felt the activity was . . . .

_____

_____

_____

Draw a picture to express your feelings about today.

Sample Parent Letter

Dear Parents,

   Recently your son/daughter took a pretest covering _____.

There were _____ skills assessed on the pretest. Because your child already

understood the skill (s) _____

_____

he/she does not have to listen to instruction on them but can do an alternate

activity.

   The alternate activities are designed to enrich, accelerate, and extend

_____ concepts for your son/daughter. He/she is not just doing

"more of the same." Your child shows a lot of responsibility and self-initiative

by working on alternate activities. You should be very proud that _____

is demonstrating such wonderful life skills.

                 Sincerely,

Helpful Hints for Implementing Curriculum Compacting

1. The teacher sets the mastery level for the standards.

2. Procedures must be established concerning the wise use of compacting time. These should be clear to students before they begin compacting. These could be developed and agreed upon by the whole class.

3. Alternate activities are never busy work. Instead, these activities must truly extend, accelerate, or enrich the curriculum. Challenge should be the emphasis.

4. Look for student activities that would be good for your compacting students. Once you are aware of this strategy, you will see such activities everywhere. Planning them well so that students can do them independently is the key to success with this strategy.

5. Students who have compacted out of regular classroom work need to be held accountable for their learning time. Use some type of Learning Log or Student Feedback Form.

6. Communication with parents is important. They need to know what compacting is, how it works, and how it affects their child.

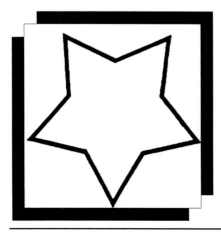

To Summarize . . .
Curriculum Compacting

➢ Curriculum compacting, developed by Dr. Joseph Renzulli and Linda Smith at the University of Connecticut, provides a structured way to find out and document what individual students already know before you begin a unit of study.

➢ The Compactor Form is a record-keeping form for documenting skills and knowledge, evidence of mastery, and alternate activities the student will work on rather than do the regular classroom work.

➢ There are many sources for alternate activities. Some suggestions are: activities included in the Teacher's Edition of your textbook, supplemental materials that come with your textbook, supplemental books that target higher-level thinking skills and activities you've used in past years that now reside in your file cabinet.

➢ Compacting students need guidelines concerning behavior and work habits. They may also need guidelines for choosing an alternate activity.

➢ "The one choice you never have is the choice to do nothing" is an essential rule for compacting students.

➢ Parents should understand what compacting is and should be informed when their child is doing curriculum compacting.

➢ Variations on curriculum compacting include 'Reverse Compacting' and 'Half and Half Compacting.'

➢ Compacting and flexible grouping can be used to divide an entire grade level for instruction during a specific unit of work.

➢ A unit with a number of specific skills can be broken down so that all students can be pre-tested on the skills. Students then compact out of whichever skills they already know within the unit of study.

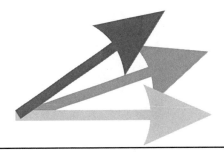

Individualized Work

Independent Study
Reliability of Sources
Records of Student Work
Learning Contracts
Resident Expert
Anchoring Activities
Learning Centers/Stations

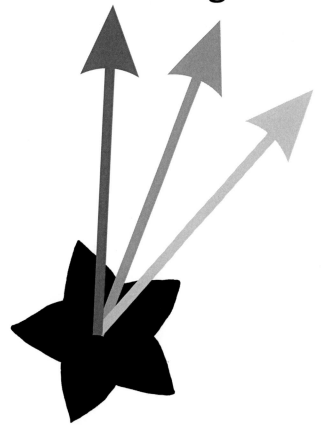

Independent Study

Independent study is a process that facilitates in-depth inquiry into an area of interest or into a topic that extends the regular curriculum. It provides an opportunity for students to develop their individual talents, expand their research skills, and explore special interests.

There are many types of independent study, from a short research report, to a more complex project, to a formal term paper. During any of these, the teacher needs to schedule times with the student for formative assessment. This often includes establishing checkpoints to assess and oversee student progress toward stated goals. Rules and guidelines for the study are essential and should be monitored by the teacher or another responsible adult such as a mentor.

Some factors to consider when students are doing independent study are:

- Developing research skills
- Determining the reliability of sources (print, e-mail, and websites)
- Evaluating types of information
- Planning long range projects
- Developing organizational skills
- Choosing products or performances to demonstrate learning

All of these will be considered either later in this chapter or in other chapters throughout this book.

It is important to realize that students are at different levels of independence in terms of being able to do independent study. Some will not know how to organize their work or what resources to use. Learning and achievement come when we move students toward greater independence a little at a time.

In this chapter, in addition to looking at various facets of developing research skills and independence in learning, we will consider several approaches to giving students individualized work.

These include:

> ➤ **Learning Contracts**

> ➤ **Resident Experts**

> ➤ **Anchoring Activities**

> ➤ **Learning Centers/Stations**

Many of the other differentiation strategies in this book also require as least some skill in doing research and independent work. **For this reason, independent learning skills are basic for students to know in order to function well in a differentiated classroom.**

Resources published by Pieces of Learning that are particularly helpful in developing skills needed to do independent study and research are:

Independent Study: Expanded with CD by Dodie Merritt
Research Book for Gifted Programs by Nancy Polette
Research Reports to Knock Your Teacher's Socks Off by Nancy Polette
Research Without Copying by Nancy Polette
Researching Adventures by Laura Magner
SMART Studying Book 2 by Frishknect and Schroeder
The Research Project Book by Nancy Polette

Reliability of Sources in Independent Study

Jon was working hard on his independent study research. He had not simply cut and pasted lots of information from websites and printed it out. That was what his friend Brad did, and Brad was ready to turn in his report. While Brad's approach was quick and easy, Jon thought that was not the way to really understand the topic.

Nor was he planning to use the research essay he found on a website that was already written and ready to be handed in, though several of his friends were going to do exactly that! Yet Jon was still concerned. He had lots of contradictory information and didn't know which of it to use. He didn't know how to organize everything or how to judge what information was reliable and what wasn't.

In an age of 'Information Glut,' all students need to develop skills in using and evaluating resources for independent study. Some students may be happy just cutting and pasting paragraphs from different sources. Others may feel like Jon, wanting to do well but not knowing how to organize information or how to be critical information consumers. These are perhaps the most essential skills in the Information Age.

More than ever before, we need to teach our students about the reliability of sources. When almost all sources were in print and were from reputable publishers, reliability was not as much of a problem. However, with the advent of websites, blogs, self-publishing, and the like, all of this has changed. Much inaccurate information is out there and available, for we live in an age where anyone can be an author and a publisher of their own work.

Students must be taught to discriminate and recognize reliable vs. poor sources of information. Information cannot be readily understood without evaluating its source and placing it in context. When researching appropriately, students will gather information from a wide variety of different sources and then create a finished product. In doing this, they must learn to use critical thinking skills. They must analyze, synthesize, and evaluate the information they gather and develop the ability to understand, appraise, and integrate information from a wide variety of sources.

When information from the Internet reinforces students' knowledge from past experiences and/or from ideas and facts they have obtained from other media (books, magazines, newspapers, CDs, commercially produced computer software, DVDs, TV, etc.) they can make the connections necessary to analyze and interpret the information. On the other hand, when information from the Internet comes in a vacuum and is not connected to other ideas and experiences, incorrect, unreliable, or biased information is more likely to be taken as truth.

There are a number of websites that give helpful guidelines for evaluating web pages. Become familiar with these and share them with your students as appropriate.

- http://www.lib.berkeley.edu/Teaching Lib/Guides/Internet/Evaluate.html
- http://www.library.jhu.edu/researchh elp/general/evaluating/
- www.alexa.com will give you information, statistics, and reviews about any specific website.

Look up the website in a directory such as www.informine.com or www.about.com or www.academicinfo.com.

Reliability of Sources
General Guidelines

It is difficult for students to judge the reliability of sources of information. In many schools, trained media specialists may give specific lessons about how to locate and use various sources. Collaborate with your media specialist as much as possible as your students start to do independent study and research of any type.

Students in the primary grades usually use the sources that are given to them. They may look in several books and on websites that have been bookmarked for them. Older students are generally more savvy in using the Internet, but are often not skilled at evaluating sources or the information they contain. Many times they click from one website to another, never noticing how the information is linked or even how they discovered a given website.

Because many students seem to be interested in merely creating a final product as fast as they possibly can, with the only goal being to turn it in to the teacher, they don't generally evaluate either their sources or the information itself.

The questions on the next three pages are guidelines for determining the reliability of sources. These include:

- Print sources
- E-mail sources
- Website sources

You may want to discuss them with your entire class or have small groups of students discuss them before starting a research project or independent study. Use these guidelines as discussion starters, and see what other guidelines your students might add.

Particularly with electronic media, new products and new methods of disseminating information come so quickly these lists may need to be updated and added to regularly.

To become good researchers, students need to know how to keep accurate records of their sources of information. This seems natural when using print sources, but it is not as easily done when using the Internet. Many students don't know how they found a certain website and often can't find it a second time. For accurate record keeping, have your students use the **Website Record Form for Students** found on page 61.

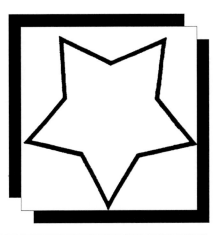

Print Sources
Questions for Students
to Consider

- What is the copyright date? Is this an updated version of an older book or article? The date something was written could affect its accuracy. Many sources become outdated quickly.

- Can you find two sources that say the same thing or give you the same information?

- Is the source a respected source in the profession or area you are researching?

- Can you verify the facts presented by asking a knowledgeable person in this field of study?

- Who is the publisher? What is the publisher's reputation? Did the author pay to have the work printed? Check with a librarian or your school media specialist to help you answer these questions.

- Is the point of view opinionated or slanted in a particular way? If so, this may not be a reliable source.

- If your source is a newspaper or magazine, is the article an editorial/opinion column or a report of the facts?

- If your source cites surveys, polls, or studies, were these funded by a person or group who wants you to see things from their point of view?

- Does the author or publisher have a political agenda or a hidden agenda? In other words, do they have a special reason for wanting you to believe the facts the way they have presented them?

- If your source is in a magazine or newspaper, is it an advertisement? You can tell if it is because this will be noted in small print somewhere on the page. An advertisement may have some good information in it, but it will almost always present a slanted point of view rather than an unbiased point of view.

E-mail Sources
Questions for Students
to Consider

- Consider the e-mail address itself. Is it connected with an institution? Some indicators are an address ending in *edu* (educational institution), *gov* (government), *org* (organization), or *mil* (military). *Net* and *com* indicate commercial services.

- What country, if any, is indicated? Be aware that people can purchase e-mail or web addresses from other countries, so this is not always a good indicator.

- Is the e-mail address linked to a web page?

- What is the source's business name, address, phone, and/or fax number?

- Will they give you the name of another person who can corroborate what they are saying?

- Can the person give you the names of some published print sources you could find that say the same thing he/she is saying?

- What are the person's qualifications and credentials? Identify these in as much detail as possible.

- Did your spam blocker reject an e-mail? If so, do not use it unless you know who it is from and have had previous contact with the person.

- Do you know why you are receiving this e-mail? Did you sign up for it or request information? If you don't know where it came from, it is probably untrustworthy.

Website Sources
Questions for Students
to Consider

- Can you find two different websites that are not linked yet say the same thing or give you the same information?

- Is the website developed by a respected source in the profession or area you are researching? Is it a reliable government agency or institution?

- Can you find the name of the organization sponsoring the website by using a search engine? What are other people saying about this organization?

- Do all of the hypertext links cited on the web page take you to internal pages on the same site? This may indicate a slanted point of view. If the links are to external sources, are these reliable?

- Does the point of view seem opinionated or slanted in a particular way? What biases or prejudice may the author have? Does it give the full story? Both sides? Does it try to be fair and balanced?

- Does the information seem likely, possible, or probable? Is it consistent or does it have contradictions?

- Can you verify the facts presented through another source?

- Does the website have a bibliography? If so, does it include books and other print resources as well as technological resources?

- If surveys, polls, or studies are cited, were these funded by a person or group who wants you to see things from their point of view? Are quotes and statistics documented?

- What are the credentials or background of the organization or person sponsoring this website?

- Is there a way to e-mail or contact that person or organization?

- When was the site created? Does it have a copyright date? When was it last updated?

- Is the site one your teacher or media specialist gave you? If not, and you found it using a search engine, what topic were you searching?

Website Record Form for Students

It's important when doing research not to just click from one website to another without having a record of how you got there. Use this form to keep a record of how you moved from one website to another. Use arrows to show which websites are linked to each other. Make notes about each website as appropriate.

Topic searched _____

Search engine used _____

First Website Visited _____

Second Website Visited _____

Third Website Visited _____

Fourth Website Visited _____

Fifth Website Visited _____

Sixth Website Visited _____

Evaluating Sources/Evaluating Information

Because our students have so much information available to them, we need to teach them how to evaluate what they read, see, and hear. This can be approached in two ways.

First, students need to consider the sources of the information they use. Answering the questions on the previous pages about Print Sources, E-mail Sources and Website Sources is a good start. The next step is to show them how to classify sources in some way. In general, sources tend to fall into three categories:

> ➤ **Respected/Historically Reliable Sources** (for example, <u>Encyclopedia Britannica</u>)

> ➤ **Generally Respected Recent Sources** (for example, Colin Powell's <u>My American Journey</u>)

> ➤ **Questionable Sources** (for example, some of the entries in *Wikipedia*)

> Have your students use the form on page 63 to classify the sources they use.

> Next, students need to examine and evaluate the information itself. Again, information tends to fall into three general categories:

> ➤ **Historically respected and accepted ideas, information, and facts** (for example, President John F. Kennedy was assassinated in Dallas, Texas, on November 22, 1963.)

> ➤ **Recent ideas still being researched and revised by experts** (for example, considering whether there was more than one gunman involved.)

> ➤ **Off-the-wall controversial ideas and information** (for example, a claim that the assassination was planned by Lyndon B. Johnson so that he could become President.)

Have your students use the form on page 64 to classify the ideas and information they use.

Doing this type of higher-level thinking will lead students to become better researchers. It also motivates them to look more deeply at their sources and the information itself, and it makes research much more exciting to do.

Evaluate and Classify Your Sources

Respected/Historically Reliable Sources	Generally respected recent sources	Questionable Sources

Evaluate and Classify Ideas and Information

Historically respected and accepted ideas, information and facts	Recent ideas still being researched and revised by experts	Off the wall controversial ideas and information

Reproducible

Records and Logs of Student Work

One of the major differences between a non-differentiated classroom and a differentiated classroom is that in a non-differentiated classroom all students are doing the same activity at the same time. This certainly makes it easy for the teacher to glance around the room and know what each student is doing. She can determine which students have finished the work and which are slow to start. She can ascertain which students are turned to the correct page or which are working on the assigned activity.

In a differentiated classroom, it is likely that students will be working on different activities at any given time. This makes it more difficult for the teacher to keep track of everyone or even to know exactly what each student is doing. For this reason, it is important for students to learn how to be accountable for their own learning, keep track of what they are doing, and have a way of communicating that to the teacher. This can be something as simple as a Daily Log or a more complex record of work on a long-term project. In either case, students and the teacher need to work together so that time is not wasted and so that the student doesn't sit for days because he doesn't understand an assignment or activity.

An individual daily log for each student to turn in while working on an independent study might look like the one below. A longer Record of Work form for long-range projects can be found on the next two pages.

Individual Daily Log

Name _____ Date _____

What I worked on today _____

_____

_____

Something I need help with is _____

_____

_____

One thing I learned is _____

_____

_____

Record of Work

Record of Work for Product or Performance

Date	Work Planned	Work Actually Done	Adjustments to Plan for next day	Reflections on my work (Difficulties, strengths, surprises)
Monday	Find books and other information on the topic at home and at the library.	Found one book at home. My mom couldn't take me to the library.	Now I need to go to the library tomorrow.	My mom was too busy and she is making me get behind. I wish I could drive.
Tuesday	Take notes from all sources. See what's on the Internet that I could use.	Went to the library and found a book and 2 news articles. Surfed the Internet but didn't see anything useful.	I need to work on the notes tomorrow.	I saw a lot of cool stuff on the Net but nothing that will help me with this report and project.
Wednesday	Begin writing rough draft. Plan visuals to go with written report.	Took notes from the books. Started making a collage.	I want to do the whole rough draft tomorrow.	My collage is good. It is turning out better than I thought. But I wish the rough draft was finished.
Thursday	Finish rough draft. Ask someone to proofread. Work on visuals.	Finished the collage.	Now I have to do the rough draft and the final report this weekend.	I hate homework on weekends. I leave the stuff I don't like to do until the last minute.
Weekend	Do final report. Finish visuals. Put together in folder.	Rough draft done. My dad proofread it. I got my folder and decorated it.	I have to do the whole final written report on Monday night.	I wish this assignment was done. My collage is the best!
Monday	Check to make sure everything is ready to be turned in tomorrow.	Written report finished. Everything is in a folder.	I am ready to turn this in.	I'm glad the teacher made us plan a "cushion day" in our projected work plan. That is the only reason this will be turned in on time.

Record of Work for Product or Performance

Date	Work Planned	Work Actually Done	Adjustments to Plan for next day	Reflections on my work (Difficulties, strengths, surprises)
Monday				
Tuesday				
Wednesday				
Thursday				
Weekend				
Monday				

Learning Contracts

A learning contract is a formalized agreement between student and teacher (and sometimes the parent) that allows a student to work on certain learning tasks or activities for an agreed-upon time.

Learning Contracts typically delineate the work the student will be doing during a unit of study. Often this work will be done independently. Activities usually involve student choices and target skills, levels of thinking, or learning styles appropriate for an individual child.

Learning Contracts for gifted students generally allow for acceleration, extensions/enrichment or both. Learning contracts for struggling students or students who are English language learners may focus on skills or knowledge they need to learn to bring them up to grade-level standards.

There are many types of Learning Contracts. Ordinarily, they list the work or study a student agrees to do. Most also include rules, working conditions, expectations for behavior, time management, and due dates. Contracts of all kinds normally include signatures. The same is true for Learning Contracts. Having both the teacher and the student sign the Learning Contract creates a formal agreement for student work. Sometimes you may want to have a parent signature as well.

Some Learning Contracts include Checkpoint Dates. These are the dates when you will look at the progress the student is making. Use Checkpoint Dates as formative assessments and to help the student stay on task. This will lessen the chances of procrastination and last minute panic!

Most rules in a Learning Contract involve at least some of the following issues:

- Expectations of the amount of work to be done
- Amount of time to be spent working on the contract at home
- Mobility that is allowed within the classroom or within the school
- Where to store unfinished work while the contract is in process
- Where to get help
- How much adult assistance is allowed
- Amount of talking allowed within the classroom or school

Designing Learning Contracts takes lots of thought and planning. Think through the questions on the next page before you develop a Learning Contract for your students. Planning is the key to implementing this strategy successfully.

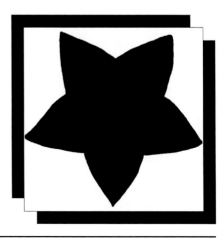

Teacher Questions
Things to Consider when Developing Learning Contracts

1. How long do you want students to work on this Learning Contract?

2. Do you want it to be connected with ongoing classroom activities or a completely independent study?

3. Is there a certain time of day that will be set aside for the students to work on Learning Contracts or will it be an 'anchoring activity;' that is, something to do when they finish the regular class work?

4. Will this contract be the alternate activity when a student is compacting the curriculum?

5. Will your Learning Contract have a number of activities from which the student may choose, or will it be a contract with only one activity stated?

6. How will the rules of the contract be written or understood?

7. Will you include Checkpoint Dates for you to check the student's ongoing work? If so, how will you structure this in the contract?

8. How will the learning activities be assessed?

9. Other considerations:

Think through these questions before designing a Learning Contract. You may want to discuss them with other teachers.

Types of Learning Contracts

There are many types of Learning Contracts. On the next four pages are examples of different types. All can be used with topics the students have chosen themselves or with topics assigned by the teacher. They are:

> **Learning Contract for Younger Students**
> This contract is very simple and is a way to start young students doing independent work using a contract. A few resources should be listed as well as three rules. More than three rules are generally lost on young children. There is one Checkpoint Date for formative assessment before the work is turned in. The verbs "Making, Writing, Doing" are easily understood by young children and are a good way to guide them in deciding what they want to do to learn more about the topic.

> **Learning Contract for Older Students (Higher Level)**
> This contract is structured in a similar way to the one for Younger Students with some important differences. The resource listing is more precise with author, title, publisher, website, etc. required. Three rules are again included along with verbs indicating the higher levels of Bloom's Taxonomy. The student should fill in what he or she wants to do based on these verbs. Two Checkpoint Dates are included for formative assessment before the final due date. There is no parent signature on the form, but this is something you may want to add.

> **Learning Contract for Older Students (Lower Level)**
> This contract is nearly identical to the one above with one significant difference. The three verbs from which the student activities originate are all from the lower levels of Bloom's Taxonomy. This contract could be given to struggling students, special needs students, or English language learners. It can be used for some students in the class while others use the contract with the higher levels of Bloom.

> **Learning Contract for a Unit of Study**
> This contract outlines the entire unit of study. It includes required activities that all students will do and then gives options for individual work. For students who need more time or more instruction in order to understand basic unit concepts and standards, there is the Remediation Option. For students who would like to explore an aspect of the topic at a higher level, there is the Acceleration Option. And for students who would like to examine a portion of the topic that was not covered (or only briefly covered) in class, there is the Extension Option. This contract is an example of a contract that could be used by every student in a differentiated classroom. Therefore, all students would be working on a contract but doing different activities within the contract's structure.

Learning Contract for Younger Students

Name _____

I want to learn about: _____

Materials/Resources I will use:

_____

_____

_____

Rules I will follow:

1. _____

2. _____

3. _____

I will show what I have learned by:

Making _____

Writing _____

Doing _____

Dates:

I will show the teacher what I have done on _____ (date)

I will finish everything by: _____ (date)

Signatures:

Student _____ Teacher _____

Parent _____

Learning Contract for Older Students

Name _____

Topic: _____

Materials/Resources (author, title, publisher, website, etc.):

_____

_____

_____

Rules I will follow while working on this contract:

1. _____

2. _____

3. _____

I will show what I have learned by: (Bloom's higher levels)

Designing _____

Analyzing _____

Evaluating _____

Dates:

First checkpoint date: _____ (date)

Second checkpoint date: _____ (date)

Final due date: _____ (date)

Signatures:

Student _____ Teacher _____

 © Pieces of Learning

Learning Contract for Older Students

Name _____

Topic: _____

Materials/Resources (author, title, publisher, website, etc.):

_____

_____

_____

Rules I will follow while working on this contract:

1. _____

2. _____

3. _____

I will show what I have learned by: (Bloom's lower levels)

Listing _____

Describing _____

Illustrating _____

Dates:

First checkpoint date: _____ (date)

Second checkpoint date: _____ (date)

Final due date: _____ (date)

Signatures:

Student _____ Teacher _____

Learning Contract for _____ **Unit of Study**

Name _____

Required Activities to be done by the Whole Class:

1. _____
2. _____
3. _____

Remediation Options *(for those who need more time or extra help with the required activities)*

1. _____
2. _____
3. _____

Acceleration Options *(for those who want to explore a topic we have studied in this unit at a higher level)*

1. _____
2. _____
3. _____

Extension Options *(for those who want to explore another aspect of this topic that we have not specifically covered in this unit)*

1. _____
2. _____
3. _____

Checkpoint and Due Dates

_____ (First checkpoint date) _____ (Second checkpoint date)

_____ (Due date)

Rules for this contract

1. _____
2. _____
3. _____

Teacher signature _____ Student signature _____

Resident Experts

School had been in session about a month. I had just finished a math lesson with my group of fifth graders, and each student was supposed to be working on the math assignment. I was getting ready for the next activity when I looked up and saw a bright-eyed boy standing beside me. Before I could say anything, he blurted out, "Do you know that the only native mammals in New Zealand are bats? There are lots of volcanoes there, and when they erupted a long time ago, the only mammals that survived were the bats. That's because they live in caves!" I was quite taken aback, but acknowledged what he had told me before telling him to go to his seat and work on his math!

About a week later, the same boy came up to me again. This time he said, "I was talking to my parents about vacation next summer. They're going to take me to Carlsbad Caverns in New Mexico. There are lots of Mexican Freetail Bats there, and you can sit and watch them leave the cave each night. I can't wait to see them!" Again, I acknowledged what he had shared with me, and then asked him to continue his regular work.

The third time he came up to me in this manner I said, "I bet you have something to tell me about bats!" He smiled broadly, and from that moment I was sure I had a Resident Expert on Bats in my class.

Like the 'Bat Boy' described above, you may have some students who are Resident Experts in an area of particular interest. These students already know a great deal about a given topic, they love the topic, and want to study it still more. For most of these students, there is little, if any, time within the school day or week to study their passion areas.

In a differentiated classroom, these Resident Experts can be given class time to study their areas of interest in depth. Many may finish regular class work early. Working on a Resident Expert study is a perfect anchoring activity (see page 78). Nearly all state standards include information gathering and research. For example:

➢ Organize and summarize ideas from multiple sources.
➢ Search multiple sources to complete research projects and reports.

Doing extended research as a Resident Expert is an excellent way to meet these standards.

Classroom Resident Experts generally have a specified time to share their information with the rest of the class. Sometimes they are asked to go to other classrooms as guest speakers on their topics of expertise.

Like any other type of independent study or individualized work, Resident Expert work should be structured in some way. This not only authenticates what the student has studied, it also gives value to the work each student has done. The Resident Expert Planning Form on page 77 provides such structure. Additionally, it helps in focusing these students on what they would like to study next in their particular area of interest or expertise.

Variations on the Resident Expert Strategy

1. When a class Resident Expert spends time working on his or her area of interest, other students may want to do the same thing. I remember a 6th grader asking me what his fellow classmate was doing. I replied that she was studying a topic of special interest to her. *"Well,"* he countered, *"Can I study something?"* What a question! We should always be happy to answer YES to such a question! These students are Secondary Resident Experts. They don't start out with much knowledge about a topic (as Resident Experts generally do), but they can learn a great deal once they begin studying an area of interest.

2. Particularly at the middle and high school level, teachers may want to allow students to choose from a list of specific content-related topics. Each student can become a Resident Expert in one topic. This allows for some in-depth study when most teachers feel they are covering everything at lightening speed.

3. Some schools develop a school database of Student Resident Experts. This is a listing of *Resident Experts* within the school who can be called upon to go to other classes and share their knowledge. Their areas of expertise may vary greatly, but they can be a wonderful resource for teachers and for other students. This is also a great experience for the students themselves. Imagine a 2nd grader who is a Resident Expert on the topic of shells being a guest speaker for a 5th grade class! In one school, the 3rd grade teachers required every student to be a Resident Expert in something. They then developed a Third Grade Yellow Pages listing all of the topics and students' names. It was distributed to every teacher in the school. These 3rd graders were in great demand all year as guest speakers in other classes.

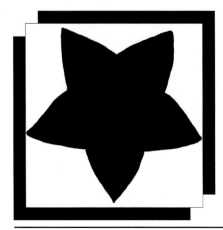

Resident Expert Planning Form

Name: _____

Topic: _____

Things I already know about this topic: (Use other side of paper if needed)

What I want to learn next about this topic:

Ways I could learn this:

My learning plan with checkpoint dates:

Activity   **Checkpoint date**

1. _____   _____

_____   _____

2. _____   _____

_____   _____

3. _____   _____

_____   _____

4. _____   _____

_____   _____

Anchoring Activities

Anchoring activities help teachers deal with the differences in the pace of learning within the classroom. They are ongoing relevant learning tasks that students automatically move to when they have completed classroom assignments.

We all know that students do not work at the same pace. When we plan a whole-class learning activity and estimate it will take the average student 30 minutes to complete it, inevitably some students will finish the assignment in 10 minutes, while others will need 45 minutes or an hour to do the same work. Because students do work and learn at different speeds, teachers need to plan for these differences. When students do not know what to do when they finish their work, they are likely to waste learning time and may become behavior problems. Having anchoring activities for your students to work on alleviates this problem.

An anchoring activity can be as simple as reading a book and doing a short book review, or as complex as a long-term independent study. The most important thing about an anchoring activity is that it should be a learning activity that can be done independently without teacher assistance.

The key to success in using anchoring activities is planning. In general, teachers know which of their students work at a fast pace. Help those students develop a list of anchoring activities they would like to do, and help them gather the materials they will need in order to do them. Many of the strategies and techniques discussed in this book can be used as anchoring activities. Additional ideas are listed below. What others can you add?

Ideas for Anchoring Activities

➢ Tic-Tac-Toe learning choices
➢ Resident Expert research
➢ Learning Centers or Stations
➢ Reading a book
➢ Logic puzzles
➢ Word puzzles (See *Think Hard* and *Think Harder* by Pam McAneny, Pieces of Learning, publisher)
➢ Crossword puzzles
➢ Geoboard activities
➢ Writing a short story or play
➢ Research about a famous person
➢ Current events
➢ Writing a poem
➢ Vocabulary research (etymologies)
➢ Glyphs (See *Researching Adventures* by Laura Magner, Pieces of Learning, publisher)
➢ Word play (See *Word Play* by R.E. Myers , Pieces of Learning, publisher)
➢ Other:

Learning Centers/Stations

Learning centers or stations are structured activities that can be done independently by individuals or groups of students. They are set up in a portion of the room or school where students can go to work on a particular task or lesson. In a differentiated classroom, not all students do the same activities in each center, and not all students go to every center.

Some teachers use the center approach for part or nearly all of their teaching. In this situation, teachers monitor progress, make sure all students understand what they are to do and are working productively, and are available to answer student questions and concerns. The more independence your students develop, the more likely you are to use the center approach as one of your major teaching strategies. This approach truly makes the teacher the facilitator of learning, the 'guide on the side' rather than the 'sage on the stage.'

Centers structure the classroom to facilitate teacher interaction with individual students or small groups. While most students are working independently, the teacher can focus on the needs of certain students. This is just not possible when presenting whole-class instruction.

Working in a learning center encourages independence and responsibility on the part of each student. It would seem that using learning centers at any grade level would be helpful in developing these traits. Ironically, learning centers are used the most in early grades (K-3) and very little in the upper grades. However, they can be used successfully in K-12 classrooms.

Centers are often developed using themes or topics. They should always be connected to the standards and lead to appropriate learning outcomes for your students.

At the elementary level, learning centers may be organized by subject area:
- Spelling center
- Reading center
- Math center
- Writing center
- Art center

At the secondary level, use centers to differentiate your content. Examples are:
- Writing center to explore different genres
- Research center for people, places, events
- Centers exploring the pros and cons of scientific topics
- Current events centers
- Individual planning for diet and physical fitness

Some learning centers focus on the multiple intelligences. For example
- Language center
- Math center
- Art center
- Hands-on center
- Music center
- Group work center
- Self-reflection center
- Nature center

Learning Centers

Teacher planning is the most important element in successful learning centers. Logistics should be well planned. Materials for each activity must be readily available. Students should understand when it is appropriate to work in the learning center and when it is not.

Consider these **guidelines** as you plan your learning centers. Think about each in light of your own situation.

A Learning Center

1. Must be structured so that the student can work independently with a minimum of direct instruction by the teacher.

2. Must fit into available physical space within your classroom or school.

3. Should be feasible given the resources of the school, grade level, or classroom.

4. Should utilize available supplies, materials, and technologies.

5. Can be displayed on a blackboard, poster, or bulletin board, or can be in a container of some type.

6. Should be visually attractive. 'Packaging' is important!

7. Must have a system for storing the students' partially finished work.

8. Can use color coding, numbers, or some other simple indicator such as a student passport, study schedule, or learning contract to guide students to the appropriate activities.

9. Can be tiered with indications of which students do which activities. (See *Tiered Activities for Learning Centers* by Karen Meador, Pieces of Learning).

10. May include activities that can be done individually and activities that can be done in pairs, trios, and/or groups of four.

Developing a good learning center or station takes both planning and set-up time. Once the planning is done, however, you have a learning activity that can last for a week or more. Many teachers plan learning centers to complement each major unit of work.

On the next few pages are samples of plans for learning centers along with blank forms to plan your own. These are:

> **Learning Center Planning Form** – Lists topic, standards, student activities (these are put on cards or in some visual format for the students to use in the center), student product, and materials needed.

> **Example of a Learning Center Plan** – Shows the above form being used to plan a learning center.

> **Example of a Tiered Learning Center** – This learning center is entitled 'Balancing Act'. It is an example taken from *Tiered Activities for Learning Centers* by Karen Meador.

> **Tiered Learning Center Planning Form** – Includes standards, objectives, materials, center preparation, student directions and ways to tier for higher-level or lower-level students.

© Pieces of Learning

Learning Center Planning Form

Theme or Topic_____

Standards/Objectives:_____

Student Activity	Product	Materials Needed

Learning Center Planning Form

Theme or Topic: Animals

Standards/Objectives: Investigate the life cycles of animals
Understand characteristics of animals and their habitats
Interpret information from a variety of resources
Research and share information on a topic

Student Activity	Product	Materials Needed
Choose three animals from the list posted in the center. Using the books in the learning center, list 5 characteristics of each animal. Then find books that have your animals as characters. Make a chart showing differences among real animals and fictional animals.	1. List of animal characteristics 2. Chart showing differences among real and fictional animals	1. List of animals 2. Fiction and non-fiction books about animals 3. Paper or poster board for chart
Make a diorama that shows an animal in its natural habitat.	Diorama	1. Shoe boxes 2. Construction paper 3. Scissors 4. Glue 5. Clay or Play-Doh 6. Books with pictures of animal habitats
Make a Venn diagram comparing and contrasting two different animals.	Venn diagram	1. Non-fiction books about different types of animals 2. Paper with blank Venn diagram
Write a short story about visiting a zoo. Include descriptions of animals you would see.	Short story	1. Books about zoos and zoo animals 2. Paper or computer for word processing
Choose an animal. Using a paper strip, draw at least five pictures of your animal illustrating stages in its life cycle. Write a sentence under each picture explaining the stages of the life cycle.	Illustration of an animal's life cycle	1. Tag board paper strips 2. Books about animal life cycles 3. Rulers
Write and illustrate a manual explaining how to take care of a pet. Include food, shelter, training, grooming, and any other details you think are important.	Written manual with pictures on Caring for a Pet that is at least 5 pages long	1. Paper or computer for word processing 2. Books on several types of pets 3. Stapler

© Pieces of Learning

Balancing Act

Standard Addressed

Science: The student uses scientific inquiry to gather information.

Objectives

1. The student will develop an understanding of the concept of balance.
2. The student will determine how weight affects balance.

Materials

1. Empty 1-pound coffee can
2. Yardstick
3. Various sizes of bulldog paper clips
4. Drawing/writing materials

Center Preparation

Turn the coffee can on its side and use masking tape to secure it to a table or desk so that it will not roll.

Student Directions

1. Balance the yardstick on the coffee can as if it were a seesaw. Draw a picture showing the location of the coffee can with the yardstick. Write the number on the yardstick that tells where the coffee can is located. For example, is the coffee can right below the number 15 on the yardstick?
2. Attach one of the paper clips to one end of the yardstick, and then balance it on the coffee can. Now what number is the coffee can below on the yardstick? Draw a second picture including the number where the coffee can is located.
3. Add another paper clip to the same end of the yardstick and find out how this extra weight affects balance. Draw a third picture.
4. Write a brief explanation of your findings.

from *Tiered Activities for Learning Centers*. ©Pieces of Learning

➤ **Tiering the Center**

➤ **Older or More Able Students**

Objectives

1. The student will develop an understanding of the concept of balance.
2. The student will consider multiple variables in an experiment.

Materials

1. Empty 1-pound coffee can
2. Cans with Various Circumferences (vegetable can, larger coffee can, etc.)
3. Wooden Ruler
4. Thin, flexible ruler or other straight edge

Student Directions

1. Create your own experiment to find out how weight affects balance using the materials provided in this center. Is it possible to balance the yardstick with varying weights on both ends?
2. Report your findings in writing.
3. What other variables besides weight could you consider in this experiment? Try at least one additional variable and report your findings.
4. Do any of these variables make a difference?

➤ **Younger or Less Able Students**

Materials

1. Same as original center (1-4 page 41)
2. Tape recorder

Student Directions

1. Balance the yardstick on the coffee can as if it were a seesaw. Draw a picture showing the location of the coffee can with the yardstick.
2. Put one of the paper clips on one end of the yardstick and then balance it on the coffee can. Draw a picture showing what happened.
3. Add another paper clip to the same end of the yardstick. Draw a third picture.
4. Tape record your description of what you did in this center and what happened.

from *Tiered Activities for Learning Centers.* ©Pieces of Learning

Tiered Learning Center Planning Form

Learning center or station _____

Standards addressed:

Objectives:

Materials:

Center preparation:

Student directions:

Tiering for lower ability students:

Tiering for higher ability students:

To Summarize . . .
Independent or Individualized Work

➤ **Independent study** provides an opportunity for students to use their unique abilities and talents and to explore areas of special interest.

➤ There are many types of independent study. All types must be appropriately guided and monitored. **Rules, guidelines, and checkpoints** are essential for the success of this approach.

➤ When they are doing any type of research, students need to know how to determine the **reliability of their sources** whether they use print, Internet, or other media. They also need to evaluate the quality of the sources and information they use.

➤ Requiring **records and logs** of individual student progress helps the teacher know how each student is progressing in his/her work. This also teaches students how to be accountable for their own learning.

➤ **Learning contracts** are formalized agreements between the teacher and a student that delineate the independent learning tasks a student will do during a unit of study. Learning contracts usually include due dates, rules, working conditions and expectations for behavior.

➤ The **Resident Expert** strategy allows students to pursue in-depth study in areas of interest to them. Resident experts can be students from all ability levels. The work is differentiated based on the interest of an individual student.

➤ **Anchoring activities** are ongoing relevant tasks that students do when they have completed the assigned work. Anchoring activities are done independently without teacher assistance.

➤ **Learning centers or stations** are pre-planned, structured activities set up in a portion of the classroom or school. Students visit learning centers to complete a specific learning task. In a differentiated classroom, not every student needs to go to every center or do every activity in the center. Learning centers can be tiered to meet the needs of both higher and lower-ability levels.

Using Learning Profiles
and
Preferences
for
Product Differentiation

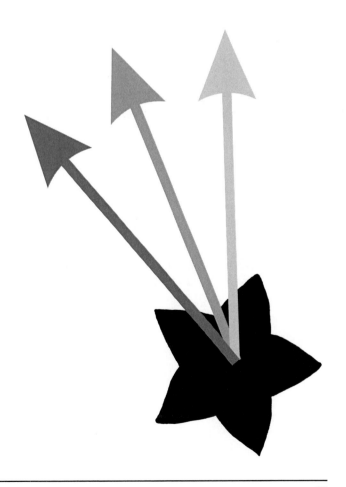

Learning Profiles and Preferences: An Overview

There are a number of different ways to discover how kids learn best. You can observe them in the classroom and see which learning activities they gravitate to or enjoy most. You can give a variety of options for learning and see which are chosen by individual students.

Using learning theories to detect your students' learning preferences is another good approach. There are a number of learning style theories as well as ways to discover favored modalities and preferred intelligences.

Developing learning profiles for individual students and designing curriculum based on how students learn is one of the best ways to differentiate instruction in the classroom. In this chapter, I have summarized and combined various learning theories in order to create a quick way for you to identify different types of learners and consider learning activities appropriate for each.

In this chapter you will find nine types of learning preferences and ten products or performances for each. Fill in the blank with your subject area content to create differentiated units of work. In the next chapter you will learn about several formats for writing differentiated units. You can use the products and performances in this chapter with any of these formats.

At the end of this chapter you will see two webs to use with students:

➤ Differentiated Activity Web
➤ Differentiated Product Web

Both of these allow for student choices and are a quick way to differentiate in any subject area.

Consult my book, *Teaching Tools for the 21st Century*, Pieces of Learning, Publisher, for a more detailed and expanded look at learning profiles and correlating student products and activities specifically based on:

➤ Learning styles
➤ Learning modalities
➤ Bloom's Taxonomy
➤ Multiple intelligences

Visual learners

- Learn by seeing, watching demonstrations
- Enjoy and learn from visual displays and colors
- Like pictures, graphic organizers, maps, story boards

Differentiated Products / Performances

Use these ideas for visual learners and fill in your own content or subject matter.

1. Make a painting of _____.

2. Draw a picture to show your ideas about _____.

3. Make a mural illustrating _____.

4. Show _____ on a map of _____.

5. Design a cartoon or comic strip about _____.

6. Make a collage of _____

7. Draw a diagram showing _____.

8. Use a visual organizer to _____.

9. Create a shape story about _____.

10. Illustrate a picture book on the subject of _____.

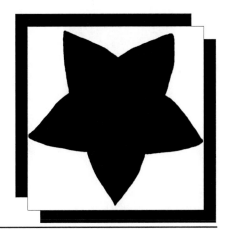

Verbal learners

- Enjoy listening but are always ready to talk
- Like music, poetry, dialogues, skits, and debates
- Learn through verbal instructions

Differentiated Products / Performances

Use these ideas for verbal learners and fill in your own content or subject matter.

1. Debate a classmate on the following topic: _____

2. Write and perform a skit about _____.

3. Do an oral report on _____.

4. Compose a poem about _____ and read it to the class.

5. Read a short story _____ (title) and summarize it.

6. Interview a person who is knowledgeable about _____.

7. Explain your point of view concerning _____.

8. Give a speech about _____.

9. Participate in a panel discussion on _____.

10. Brainstorm a list of _____.

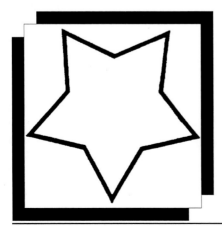

Kinesthetic learners

- Learn by hands-on experiences
- Like working with materials, manipulatives and tools
- Remember what they have done more than what they have seen or heard

Differentiated Products / Performances:

Use these ideas for kinesthetic learners and fill in your own content or subject matter.

1. Design a game about _____.

2. Make a set of puppets and put on a puppet show depicting _____.

3. Create a dance that shows _____.

4. Make a scrapbook of _____.

5. Write and perform a skit about _____.

6. Do a pantomime showing how _____.

7. Create a carving or sculpture of _____.

8. Construct a model of _____.

9. Make a diorama that illustrates _____.

10. Invent a set of manipulatives that _____.

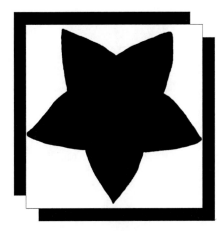

Technological learners

- Know how to use technological tools without formal instruction
- Expertise in using digital cameras, video production tools, smart boards, computer technologies, etc.
- Understand how to integrate various technologies

Differentiated Products / Performances:

Use these ideas for technological learners and fill in your own content or subject matter.

1. Do a computer-generated report with graphics illustrating _____.

2. Do a presentation about _____ using an interactive whiteboard.

3. Create a PowerPoint presentation to explain _____.

4. Make and edit a video about _____.

5. Review and evaluate ____ (number) websites about _____.

6. Set up interactive video conferencing concerning _____.

7. Do an e-mail interview with _____.

8. Create a slide show from digital pictures to demonstrate _____.

9. Produce an in-house TV or radio show that explains _____.

10. Write a report about _____ using a word processor.

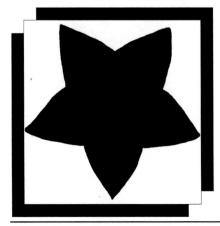

Musical/Rhythmic learners

- Have the ability to communicate through music and poetry
- Can compose and/or perform musically
- Have a natural rhythm, beat and harmony

Differentiated Products / Performances:

Use these ideas for musical/rhythmic learners and fill in your own content or subject matter.

1. Write and sing a song about _____.

2. Do a choral reading of _____ (name of poem or passage).

3. Write a poem explaining _____.

4. Write and perform a rap concerning _____.

5. Do a musical performance to illustrate _____.

6. Produce a musical video about _____.

7. Write and sing musical advertisement for _____.

8. Make up words to well-known tunes to show what you know about _____.

9. Create musical mnemonics to help you remember _____.

10. Compose and read aloud a diamond poem about _____.

Note: A diamond poem starts with one word, second line has two words, etc. with the longest number of words in the middle of the poem. The number of words then goes in reverse order.

Imagine
Writing poetry
Shaped like diamonds
With many expressive words
Conveying my feelings
Using creativity
Forever

For more information about using music in the classroom, log onto www.learningfromlyrics.org.

Logical/Mathematical learners

- Think in a logical, ordered, sequential way.
- Use reasoning and logic to solve problems
- Use numbers effectively
- See logical patterns, statements and relationships

Differentiated Products / Performances:

Use these ideas for logical/mathematical learners and fill in your own content or subject matter

1. Make a graph to show _____.

2. Outline the steps for _____.

3. Observe _____ and collect data about it.

4. Create a time line of _____.

5. Solve several logic puzzles that focus on _____.

6. Categorize the elements of _____.

7. Find and record patterns in _____.

8. Compare and contrast _____ to _____.

9. Construct a chart that demonstrates _____.

10. Make a Venn diagram showing similarities and differences in _____.

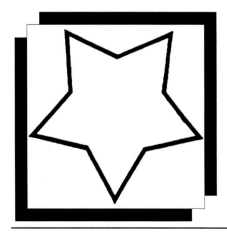

Naturalist learners

- Can create categories and sort/index items accordingly
- Are able to recognize and make distinctions between things in nature
- Observe things in nature others would miss

Differentiated Products / Performances:

Use these ideas for naturalist learners and fill in your own content or subject matter

1. Develop a science project to prove or disprove _____.

2. Organize a field trip to _____ (somewhere focusing on plants or animals).

3. Make a shadow box to display _____.

4. Create a terrarium.

5. Build a school nature trail.

6. Read and do a book report on _____. (Fiction book with "out-of-door" adventures)

7. Dissect _____. Take detailed notes on each step of the process.

8. Do an experiment to find out _____.

9. Create categories to classify information in _____ (any subject area).

10. Make a collection of _____.

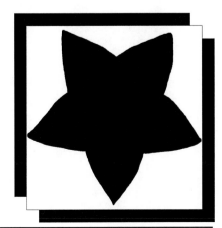

Intrapersonal/Reflective learners

- Recognize their own strengths and weaknesses
- Learn from successes and failures
- Plan for and uses suitable organization and study skills
- Understand their own hopes, dreams, aspirations, and emotions

Differentiated Products / Performances:

Use these ideas for intrapersonal/reflective learners and fill in your own content or subject matter.

1. Keep a journal or diary telling about _____.

2. Do an assessment of your strengths and weakness and make a self-improvement plan.

3. Write a reflective poem expressing your feelings about _____.

4. Design a Culture poster showing things of importance in your family or your culture.

5. Choose an independent study topic and become a resident expert on it.

6. Plan a long-range project on _____ and break up the large task into smaller parts.

7. Write an autobiography of your life focusing on _____.

8. Make a list of things that interest you and link them to topics we are studying or have studied in class.

9. Brainstorm a list of possible solutions to _____ (any problem). Decide on a plan of action.

10. Make a plan for _____.

Interpersonal / Group Oriented learners

- Work well as members of groups
- Are able to lead and persuade others
- Respond appropriately to both verbal and non-verbal cues from others
- Consider advice and opinions of others when making a decision

Differentiated Products / Performances:

Use these ideas for interpersonal/group oriented learners and fill in your own content or subject matter.

1. Debate with a classmate: _____.

2. In a group, develop a plan for _____.

3. Brainstorm possible answers to the question: _____.

4. As a group, write a story focusing on _____.

5. Do an email interview with an expert to find out about _____.

6. With a partner, design _____.

7. Conduct a class meeting to decide _____.

8. Develop a game about _____ and play it with a partner.

9. Design a group symbol / logo for your class.

10. Plan and implement a project to help people in your community.

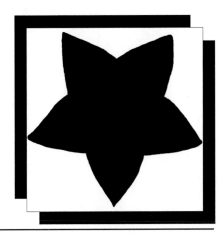

Differentiated Activities Web

Design a newspaper front page to give some facts

Make a list of careers that exist

Make a television and a scroll story with facts and pictures

Make a fold-out chart of new words or expressions to add to your vocabulary

Make a poster that teaches one or more facts

Make a wordfind

Design a travel brochure

Write your own song—or find songs about your subject

Draw and color a mini-mural Label the facts

Take a survey and make a graph

Construct a diorama - include 6 facts on an index card

Make a model of plaster, clay, wood, or soap

Make up a quiz with 10 questions and answers

Write a letter for collecting information

Make a chart to show similarities or differences

Write a report and draw a picture

ACTIVITIES

Make a dictionary with pictures and definitions

Draw and label a map

Draw a time line

Design a mobile with at least 6 facts

Make a cartoon strip to tell some facts

Create a book cover to tell about your subject

Design a mini-book

Make a scrapbook

Create a montage

Design a magazine with facts and pictures

Design a bookmark with 3 facts

Construct a game with at least 10 facts

Write a poem and illustrate it.

Design a collage

Make a flipbook

Make a crossword puzzle

Make 10 Trivia cards

Make a list of books about your subject

Reproducible

Differentiated Products Web

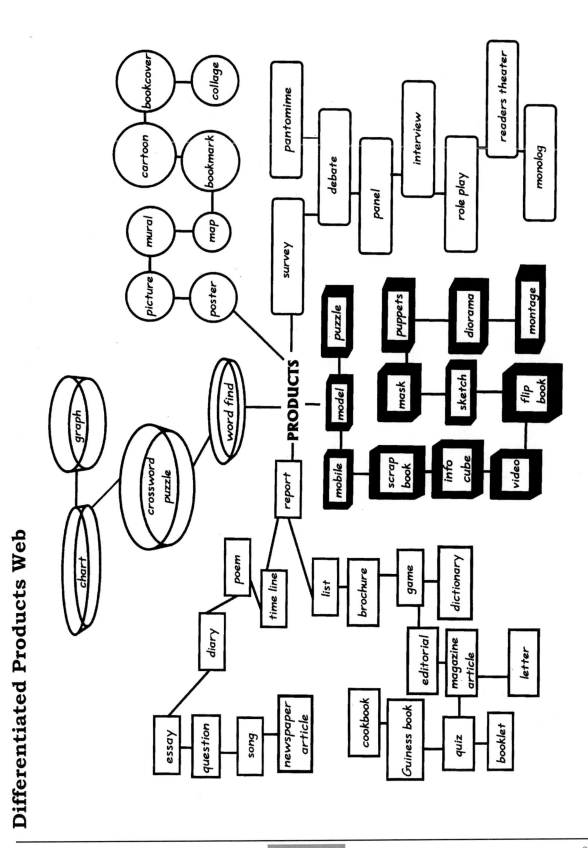

To Summarize . . .
Using Learning Profiles and
Preferences for Product Differentiation

➤ Using individual students' learning profiles and preferences is a good approach for differentiating instruction.

➤ Learning profiles can be based on learning styles, learning modalities and multiple intelligences and can use all levels of Bloom's Taxonomy.

➤ Types of learners include: Visual learners, Verbal learners, Kinesthetic learners, Technological learners, Musical/Rhythmic learners, Logical/Mathematical learners, Naturalist learners, Intrapersonal/Reflective learners, and Interpersonal/Group-oriented learners.

➤ There are differentiated products and performances to use with each type of learner.

➤ Differentiated Activity Webs and Differentiated Product Webs can be used for differentiation by providing students with many different choices to show what they have learned.

➤ Consider a school wide or district wide plan for articulating products K-12. Decide which products should students typically learn to do at different grade levels.

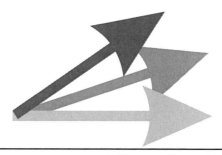

Formats for Writing Differentiated Lessons and Units

Individual Lesson Plan (ILP™)
Tic-Tac-Toe
Tiered Lessons and Units
Encounter Lessons

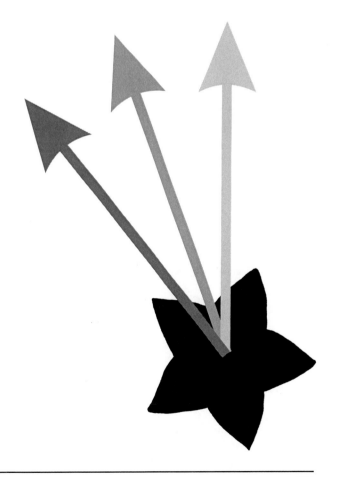

Introduction: Formats for Writing Differentiated Lessons and Units

Almost all differentiation strategies require careful and thoughtful planning. At the same time, this planning cannot be too arduous or time consuming because it would then be impossible for teachers to do it! In this chapter, we will examine four practical formats you can use to plan differentiated units and lessons. Each has a specific purpose and function. Decide which would be most useful to you and which one you might like to start using first.

> The **Individual Lesson Plan (ILP™)** format structures a unit of work outlining both Teacher Required and Student Choice activities. Differentiation is provided by the student choice activities which can be categorized in a number of different ways.

> The **Tic-Tac-Toe** format gives students nine different activity choices, usually focusing on a specific theme or topic. Students are generally required to complete three activities out of the nine. Choices can be set up in a variety of different ways.

> **Tiered lessons or units** are most often used in mixed-ability classes. All students work toward the same standards or objectives but at different levels of readiness or ability.

> **Encounter lessons** frequently introduce a unit of work. They are comprised of a series of Leading Questions based on a simulation or fictional scenario. These questions develop both listening and creative thinking skills. Differentiated Extenders follow the Leading Questions and give students choices of differentiated assignments for the lesson or unit.

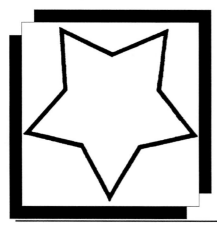

Individual Lesson Plan (ILP™) Format

*The **ILP™** format is a graphic organizer used to design a unit of work. It organizes standards-based learning activities so that students have a choice as to which activities they want to do. These choices can be based on student Learning Profiles or Preferences such as learning styles, learning modalities or multiple intelligences.*

You can use any of the Learning Profiles and suggested Products/Performances listed in the last chapter to create categories and activities for an **ILP™**.

Student Choice Activities can also be based on subject areas, Bloom's Taxonomy, different aspects of the standard or content, or any other way that creates categories of student choices. Even though it outlines an entire unit of work, this format is called an **Individual Lesson Plan** because each student uses it to create his or her own individual lesson plan for the unit by choosing one or more of the *Student Choice Activities.*

The **ILP™** form lists the standards addressed in the unit, as well as all of the unit activities. In addition to *Student Choice Activities*, which are listed on the left hand side of the form, the upper right hand quadrant of the **ILP™** lists the *Teacher Required Activities* that all students must do. This combination of Student Choice and Teacher Required activities makes up a differentiated unit of work.

The first *Teacher Required Activity* should be an independent activity for students. Students can work on this activity while the teacher is meeting with small groups of students regarding each *Student Choice* activity.

The other *Teacher Required Activities* generally are teacher directed whole class activities that will be done during the course of the unit.

The *Student Choice Activities* are numbered and the students write the numbers to indicate their choices on the bottom middle block of the **ILP™** form. On the next block to the right, each student lists the products or performances he or she will produce as a result of doing their chosen activities. The block on the far right shows the due dates for each of the individual *Student Choice* activities. On page 106 you will see a sample ILP unit on Natural Disasters. On the next page, 107, you will see the same ILP showing how the student choices are indicated.

I underline and boldface the products or performances in each of the *Student Choice Activities*. I find this helps students focus more quickly and understand exactly what they are required to do for each choice.

The teacher decides how many *Student Choice Activities* each student must do. Often teachers begin by requiring students to make two choices, each from a different category. If students finish early, they can make an additional choice.

To know which activities each of the students in your class has chosen, use the **Activity Chart** to record the choices each student makes. Call the roll and have each student answer with the numbers of his or her choices. My policy is that once the choices are recorded on the **Activity Chart**, students cannot change their minds. This encourages careful selection and teaches both commitment and responsibility.

See the example **Activity Chart** on page 112. Use the blank Activity Chart (page 113) to record your students' choices. You can also customize the blank form on the CD.

Use the **Activity Chart** to find out which students have chosen the same activity. Meet with all the students who are doing the same activity to review assessment criteria, due dates, etc. For some choices (such as a skit or debate) these students will need to work together. Meet with small groups of students for each of the *Student Choice Activities*. You can write the due dates for each activity on the **Activity Chart**. While you are doing this, students you are not currently meeting with should be working on *Teacher Required Activity #1*.

Plan the due dates carefully. Activities such as debates or oral reports need class time for preparation and presentation. Make sure everything is not due on the same day! This avoids student procrastination and makes grading less overwhelming for you. It helps to distribute these events throughout the week or weeks the students are working. It also assures oral reports and other classroom presentations are spaced over several days.

I generally use an **ILP™ Unit Planner** to think through the Essential Questions, state standards and possible unit activities before I begin writing the unit on the **ILP™** form. On the next page you will find my **ILP™ Unit Planner** for my unit on Natural Disasters. The activities indicated by ** are the ones I decided to use as *Teacher Required Activities* for everyone to do.

If you teach K-2 students, you may want to use a simplified version of the **ILP™** form with only four choices indicated. A blank copy of this form is on page 111.

In the next several pages of this chapter you will see:

➢ ILP™ Unit Planner for Natural Disasters unit
➢ ILP™ unit format for Natural Disasters unit
➢ ILP™ unit format for Natural Disasters unit with student choices indicated
➢ Steps to Develop an ILP™
➢ Blank ILP™ Unit Planner
➢ Blank ILP™ unit format
➢ Blank ILP™ unit format for K-2 students
➢ Sample Activity Chart
➢ Blank Activity Chart

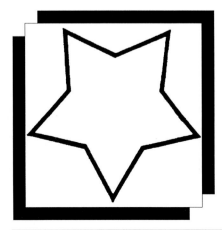

ILP™ Unit Planner

Topic or Theme: **Natural Disasters**

What do I want my students to know about this topic?
What are the essential questions we want to answer? What are the Big Ideas?

- Natural disasters occur often throughout the earth.
- Natural disasters affect people's lives.
- We can predict some natural disasters and may be able to change their outcomes.

What state standards/objectives are we working to meet?

- Understand how natural disasters can cause changes on earth.
- Evaluate the effects of natural disasters
- Present information in a variety of forms..
- Use print and non-print sources to locate information

Possible Student Activities	Product/Performance	Category/Preference
1. Model of a volcano showing the area of destruction	Model	Kinesthetic
2. Compare/contrast earthquakes and tsunamis	Venn diagram	Visual
3. Hurricane map showing path of Katrina and Rita in 2005	Map	Visual
4. Research a major natural disaster that has occurred in the past 5 years.	Written/oral report	Verbal
5. Write about the effects of a hurricane, earthquake or flood on one town or family.	Newspaper article	Verbal
**6. Read basic information about natural disasters in science book.	Answers to questions Class discussion	Verbal
**7. Guest speaker who has lived through a natural disaster	Listen and ask questions Write thank you note	Verbal
8. Slide show/photo montage showing natural disasters and information about them	Slide show/photo montage	Technological
9. Information cube about a natural disaster and its effects	Information cube	Kinesthetic
10. WebQuest about a natural disaster	WebQuest	Technological
**11. Class map and bulletin board showing natural disasters around the world and their effects	Map & bulletin board

Kinesthetic | Visual/ |

Individual Lesson Plan – Natural Disasters

Required Activities Teacher's Choice	Product/Performance Required	Assessment – Required Activities
1. Read science book chapter to learn basic information about natural disasters. Answer assigned questions.	1. Answers to questions from science book	1. Accurate answers / All questions completed
2. Listen to guest speaker who has lived through a natural disaster. Write him a thank you note telling what you learned from his talk.	2. Thank you note	2. Correct letter format / Neatly written / Correct spelling, grammar and punctuation / Tells at least 3 things you learned
3. Contribute information and pictures to the class map and bulletin board on natural disasters.	3. Portions of map and/or bulletin board information	3. At least one picture for bulletin board and one piece of written information for map

Standards/Objectives: Understand how natural disasters can cause changes on the earth / Evaluate the effects of natural disasters / Present information in a variety of forms / Use print and non-print sources to locate information

Student Choices in Ways to Learn	Product/Performance Student Choice	Due Dates Student Choice Activities
Visual ____		
Verbal ____		
Kinesthetic ____		
Technological ____		

© Carolyn Coil, www.carolyncoil.com

ACTIVITIES – STUDENT CHOICES

Visual

1. Make a **Venn diagram** comparing and contrasting earthquakes and tsunamis.

2. Use a **map** to plot the paths of Hurricanes Rita and Katrina in 2005. What conclusions can you make from looking at your map? Write a **paragraph** explaining your thoughts.

Verbal

3. Use at least three different sources to research any major disaster that has occurred in the past five years. Do a **written report** and a 5 minute **oral report** for the class. Include a bibliography.

4. Write a **newspaper article** describing the effects of a major disaster on one town or family. Include who, what, when, where, why and how. Be historically accurate.

Kinesthetic

5. Choose an active volcano from any part of the world. Construct a **model** of this volcano showing the area of destruction when it is erupting. Include buildings, animals and people in your model if the area of destruction has these. **Label** your model with its name, country and other important facts.

6. Design an **information cube** about one of these: Tsunami, Earthquake, Tornado, Hurricane or Flood Include: Locations, Definition, Effects on People Destruction Caused, Historic Disasters and Other Facts.

Technological

7. Develop a **slide show** or **photo montage** showing natural disasters and information about each. Include at least four types of disasters. Use Internet sources to develop your product.

8. Complete a **WebQuest** on natural disasters. Print out your work or keep notes about what you learned at each website as you did the WebQuest.

Individual Lesson Plan – Natural Disasters

Required Activities Teacher's Choice	Product/Performance Required	Assessment – Required Activities
1. Read science book chapter to learn basic information about natural disasters. Answer assigned questions.	1. Answers to questions from science book *(Due date written here)*	1. Accurate answers All questions completed
2. Listen to guest speaker who has lived through a natural disaster. Write him a thank you note telling what you learned from his talk.	2. Thank you note *(Due date written here)*	2. Correct letter format Neatly written Correct spelling, grammar and punctuation Tells at least 3 things you learned
3. Contribute information and pictures to the class map and bulletin board on natural disasters.	3. Portions of map and/or bulletin board information *(Due date written here)*	3. At least one picture for bulletin board and one piece of written information for map

Standards/Objectives: Understand how natural disasters can cause changes on the earth
Evaluate the effects of natural disasters
Present information in a variety of forms
Use print and non-print sources to locate information

Student Choices in Ways to Learn	Product/Performance Student Choice	Due Dates Student Choice Activities
Visual ____		
Verbal __4__	4. *Newspaper article*	*(Due date written here)*
Kinesthetic __6__	6. *Information cube*	*(Due date written here)*
Technological ____		

ACTIVITIES – STUDENT CHOICES

Visual

1. Make a <u>Venn diagram</u> comparing and contrasting earthquakes and tsunamis.

2. Use a <u>map</u> to plot the paths of Hurricanes Rita and Katrina in 2005. What conclusions can you make from looking at your map? Write a <u>paragraph</u> explaining your thoughts.

Verbal

3. Use at least three different sources to research any major disaster that has occurred in the past five years. Do a <u>written report</u> and a 5 minute <u>oral report</u> for the class. Include a bibliography.

4. Write a <u>newspaper article</u> describing the effects of a major disaster on one town or family. Include who, what, when, where, why and how. Be historically accurate.

Kinesthetic

5. Choose an active volcano from any part of the world. Construct a <u>model</u> of this volcano showing the area of destruction when it is erupting. Include buildings, animals and people in your model if the area of destruction has these. <u>Label</u> your model with its name, country and other important facts.

6. Design an <u>information cube</u> about one of these: Tsunami, Earthquake, Tornado, Hurricane or Flood Include: Locations, Definition, Effects on People Destruction Caused, Historic Disasters and Other Facts.

Technological

7. Develop a <u>slide show</u> or <u>photo montage</u> showing natural disasters and information about each. Include at least four types of disasters. Use Internet sources to develop your product.

8. Complete a <u>WebQuest</u> on natural disasters. Print out your work or keep notes about what you learned at each website as you did the WebQuest.

Steps to Develop an ILP™

Note: Use the ILP™ Unit Planner found on the next page for steps 1-6 below. Use the ILP™ form on the following page for steps 7-10 below.

___1. Decide on a major theme or topic for the unit.

___2. Generate a unit rationale, a broad list of essential questions, objectives, and outcomes, and the enduring understandings you hope will result from the unit.

___3. List unit objectives/outcomes and state standards for the unit.

___4. Brainstorm a list of possible unit activities. Use your textbook, supplemental resources, Internet websites, and other teachers to help generate ideas.

___5. Categorize each activity according to learning preferences/profiles (see Chapter 5), content areas or in any other category you want.

___6. Decide which will be Student Choice activities and which will be required of all students.

___7. Use the Individual Lesson Plan (ILP™) format to organize your unit activities.

___8. Include one independent activity in the activities required of all students. List this activity first in the 'Required Activities – Teacher's Choice' section of the ILP™. This will be what all students can work on while you are meeting with small groups of students and discussing their Student Choice activities.

___9. Write all Teacher Required Activities in the upper right hand quadrant of the ILP™. Include products or performances and assessment criteria for each.

___10. Write all Student Choice activities in consecutive numerical order for easy reference. This way, you can keep a record of which students have chosen which activity by recording the number of the activity on the Activity Chart.

___11. Find or develop resources and materials needed for the unit.

___12. Develop assessments to assess unit objectives, outcomes, and standards. You could develop complete rubrics, mini-rubrics, tests or quizzes, observation logs, charts, and a host of other assessment instruments. (See Chapter 7.)

___13. As you would with any unit, develop daily lesson plans based on your unit plan.

ILP™ Unit Planner

Topic or Theme_____

What do I want my students to know about this topic? What are the essential questions we want to answer? What are the Big Ideas?

- _____
- _____
- _____
- _____

What state standards are we working to meet?

- _____
- _____
- _____
- _____

Student Activities	Product/ Performance	Learning Preference/ Category
1. _____	_____	_____
2. _____	_____	_____
3. _____	_____	_____
4. _____	_____	_____
5. _____	_____	_____
6. _____	_____	_____
7. _____	_____	_____
8. _____	_____	_____
9. _____	_____	_____
10. _____	_____	_____
11. _____	_____	_____

Individual Lesson Plan –

Required Activities Teacher's Choice	Product/Performance Required	Assessment – Required Activities

Standards/Objectives:

Student Choices in Ways to Learn	Product/Performance Student Choice	Due Dates Student Choice Activities
Choice Category #1 ___		
Choice Category #2 ___		
Choice Category #3 ___		
Choice Category #4 ___		

Carolyn Coil, www.carolyncoil.com

ACTIVITIES – STUDENT CHOICES

Choice Category #1	Choice Category #2

Choice Category #3	Choice Category #4

ILP™ for Primary Students

Title of Lesson _____

Standards _____

_____

_____

Visual	**Kinesthetic**
Technological	**Auditory/Verbal**

Activity Chart

Student Choice Activities

Students' Names	1	2	3	4	5	6	7	8
Alicia		✓			✓			
Carlos				✓			✓	
Danielle	✓					✓		
Evan			✓					✓
Edwardo				✓		✓		
Gina		✓					✓	
Heather					✓		✓	
Jim			✓			✓		
Kara	✓							✓
Maria			✓			✓		
Mark		✓			✓			
Nathan	✓					✓		
Ophra			✓					✓
Paul		✓				✓		
Pedro				✓			✓	
Quintan	✓							✓
Rachel				✓		✓		
Rusty					✓		✓	
Sarah	✓			✓				
Taneka		✓						✓
Tom				✓			✓	

Using this chart helps teachers organize a differentiated classroom. Each student in this example chose 2 activities from the 8 Student Choice Activities available. Each child's choices are recorded by using the number that corresponds to the activity.

The teacher meets with each group of students. At this time, review the assessment criteria, explain the activity, and schedule the due date. Record the due date on the chart and also write it in the teacher's plan book. If the activity is one that requires students working together, review behavioral guidelines with the students involved.

Activity Chart

Student Choice Activities

Students' Names	1	2	3	4	5	6	7	8

Notes

Tic-Tac-Toe Learning Activities

The Tic-Tac-Toe (sometimes referred to as 'Think-Tac-Toe') is a graphic organizer for student choice activities. Choices of learning activities are listed on a Tic-Tac-Toe grid. Tic-Tac-Toes are great to use in learning centers, curriculum compacting, or as anchoring activities. They can form the basis for a unit of work or can function as extensions of the required curriculum. This is one of the easiest ways to organize student choice activities and is very user-friendly. For these reasons, using a Tic-Tac-Toe is often how teachers start differentiating in their classrooms.

The Tic-Tac-Toe format gives students some choice of learning activities, but also gives teachers some control in structuring the choices. If you give students a list of nine choices and ask them to choose three without using the Tic-Tac-Toe, many students will choose the three easiest, or the three requiring no writing.

On the other hand, with the Tic-Tac-Toe format, you can be sure that any set of choices will include a variety of types of activities. You can also make sure that no matter how the choices are set up, your students will be completing activities that address the standards.

The Tic-Tac-Toe format is extremely versatile and can be used in any subject area with any age or grade level. While students usually complete products or performances in a Tic-Tac-Toe, the nine choices can be as simple as nine math word problems or nine vocabulary/spelling activities that can be chosen week after week to be done with different words.

I find that students pay more attention and make better choices when I underline and boldface the product or performance required for each Tic-Tac-Toe activity. This also helps me make sure I have been clear about my expectations.

Student choices in a Tic-Tac-Toe can be set up in many different ways:

➢ Students choose three activities as they would when playing Tic-Tac-Toe: three across, three down or three on the diagonal. **(Fairy Tales example)**

➢ Activities in the Tic-Tac-Toe grid can be based on learning preferences such as multiple intelligences, learning styles, learning modalities or Bloom's taxonomy. **(Fractions, Decimals, and Percents example)**

➢ The middle square (#5) is required for all students. Any set of three-in-a-row choices must include #5. **(Julius Caesar example)**

➢ Three different parts of a topic or standard are included on the Tic-Tac-Toe. Each row has activities based on one part. Students must choose one activity from each row of the Tic-Tac-Toe. **(Human Body example)**

➢ The Tic-Tac-Toe can be tiered, with the easiest activities on the top row, more difficult in the middle row and most difficult on the bottom row. **(Civil Rights Movement example)**

➢ The middle square (#5) is required for all students. The top row has the easiest activities, the middle row (#4 and #6) is more difficult and the bottom row is the most difficult. In addition to doing #5, students can choose to do all three activities in the top row, the two in the middle row or one from the bottom row. **(World War II example)**

The six examples of Tic-Tac-Toes on the following pages are based on each of the patterns discussed above. After you have looked at the examples, read the step-by-step directions for writing Tic-Tac-Toes. Then use the blank form to write your own.

Fairy Tales Tic-Tac-Toe Student Choice Activities

Standards/Objectives: Identifies plot, character and setting in stories
read, written or performed
Identifies themes and lessons in fairy tales, folk tales
or fables

1. **Draw or paint** your favorite fairy tale character. List five character traits for this character, put them on an index card and attach it to your picture.	2. Create a **story board** showing the main events in a fairy tale.	3. Write and perform a **skit** taking the theme of a fairy tale and putting it into life today.
4. Retell a fairy tale either as a **narrative poem** or as a **lyric poem**.	5. Write a **letter** to a friend explaining a lesson from a fairy tale that applies to your own life.	6. Make a fairy tale **collage** showing the setting for at least three fairy tales. Include both words and pictures in your collage.
7. Brainstorm a **list** of 10 character traits. Then **identify** at least three fairy tale characters with each trait.	8. Design a **comic strip** with characters from at least three different fairy tales. Make the plot of your comic strip realistic for the characters you have chosen.	9. Make a **Venn diagram** comparing and contrasting yourself and a fairy tale character.

I/we chose activities # _____, #_____, and #_____.

Name _____ Due dates _____, _____, _____

Fractions, Decimals, & Percents
Tic-Tac-Toe Student Choice Activities

Standards/Objectives: Uses fractions, decimals and percents interchangeably
Compares and orders whole numbers, integers, fractions and decimals

1. Use a **visual organizer** to compare and contrast fractions, decimals and percents. (Visual)	2. Make a five minute **oral report** explaining how to convert percentages to fractions and decimals. Use visuals in your presentation. (Verbal)	3. Convert a **recipe** that uses fractions into decimals and percents. Display the recipe and **cook** the food to share with your classmates. (Kinesthetic)
4. Create a **spreadsheet** of a budget with at least ten items. Each item should be in dollar (decimal) amounts. Identify the percentage of the budget spent on each item. (Technological)	5. Write and perform a **poem** or **rap** about fractions, decimals and percents and how they work interchangeably. (Musical/Rhythmic)	6. Make a **chart** comparing fractions, decimals and percents. (Logical/Mathematical)
7. Research an environmental topic of interest such as endangered species or global warming. Write a **report** of your findings using fractions, decimals or percents. (Naturalist)	8. Write a **journal** or **diary** of a day in your life without fractions or decimals. Include at least 10 things that would be different. (Intrapersonal/Reflective)	9. In a group with at least two other students, **discuss** real life situations where you use fractions, decimals or percents. Make a **list** of at least 10 uses and **act** these out for the class. (Interpersonal/Group)

I/we chose activities # _____, #_____, and #_____.

Name _____ Due dates _____, _____, _____

Julius Caesar Tic-Tac-Toe
Student Choice Activities

Standards/Objectives: Applying reading to historical background
Comprehension and interpretation of character development
and motivation

1. Create a **map** of the Roman Empire during the time of Caesar. Show which areas he conquered and major cities of the ancient world.	**2.** Write a **poem** that reflects Brutus' inner conflict before he decided to join the conspiracy against Caesar.	**3.** Take part in a **debate** over whether the killing of Julius Caesar was justified. Defend your position with facts from historical sources and ideas from the Shakespearean play.
4. Write and present Caesar's funeral **speech** as it might have been given by Octavius instead of Antony. Remember that Octavius was a teenager at the time of Caesar's death.	**5. (Required activity)** Read Shakespeare's play "Julius Caesar" and participate in class discussion. Write a final **essay** discussing the character motivation of either Caesar or Brutus.	**6.** Make a **Venn diagram** comparing and contrasting the motives of Cassius and Brutus.
7. Create a **brochure** advertising Rome in 44 BC. Include food, lodging and entertainment. Be historically accurate.	**8.** Do a **PowerPoint presentation** summarizing the motivations of five different characters in the play "Julius Caesar."	**9.** Write the **lead story** for a Roman newspaper in 44 BC on the day of Caesar's assassination. Include a headline and answer the questions who, what, when, why and how.

I/we chose activities # _____, #_____, and #_____.

Name _____ Due dates _____, _____, _____

Human Body
Tic-Tac-Toe Student Choice Activities

Standards/Objectives: Identifies major body systems and their functions
Names and describes important parts of the body

1. Create a two minute **public service announcement** that addresses things people can do to their bodies that have a negative influence on the skeletal or muscular system or both. Make this announcement in your class or to the entire school during the time for school wide announcements. (Skeletal & Muscular systems)	2. Make a **poster** showing five different exercises that address five different muscles. For each exercise include: - Name of exercise - Name of muscle - Illustration of muscle - Illustration of exercise - Written steps to perform the exercise (Skeletal & Muscular systems)	3. Visit www.medtropolis.com. Click on the Skeletal System section and put together a **virtual skeleton** successfully. Print out your work. (Skeletal & Muscular systems)
4. Make a **graph** showing the percentages of red blood cells, white blood cells and platelets in blood. Write an **explanation** of the function of each. (Circulatory system)	5. Draw a **diagram** showing how the circulatory system works. Label all major parts. (Circulatory system)	6. Research diseases of the circulatory system such as angina, high blood pressure, heart disease, or heart attacks. Do a three minute **oral report** explaining the causes of these diseases and how they can be prevented. (Circulatory system)
7. Write a **paragraph** explaining how the digestive and excretory systems are related to one another. Include a diagram. (Digestive & Excretory systems)	8. Write a **short story** describing life without teeth or gums. Include effects on the digestive and excretory systems. (Digestive & Excretory systems)	9. Create a set of ten **interview questions** about the digestive and excretory systems. Interview a doctor or nurse and write down their **answers** to your questions. (Digestive & Excretory systems)

I/we chose activities # _____, #_____, and #_____.

Name _____   Due dates _____, _____, _____

Reproducible   © Pieces of Learning

Civil Rights Movement Tic-Tac-Toe Student Choice Activities

Standards/Objectives: Understand the importance of the Civil Rights movement in U.S. history

Evaluate ways individuals and groups can change history

1. Make a **time line** showing 10 major events in the Civil Rights movement from 1954-1968. (Easiest)	2. Make a **bulletin board** of 5 important Civil Rights court cases. Include pictures and important details. (Easiest)	3. Choose a significant person in the Civil Rights movement. Find 3 websites about this person. **List** each website and write a **short summary** of the information found in each. (Easiest)
4. Choose a significant person in the Civil Rights movement. Prepare a list of **10 questions** you would like to ask this person. Do research to find the **answers** and write them down **in interview format**. (More Difficult)	5. Develop a detailed **chart** showing at least 5 major differences in daily life for blacks and whites during the Jim Crow era. Based on this information, write a **paragraph** highlighting your conclusions and ideas about this era. (More Difficult)	6. Create **Jeopardy questions** about important people and events of the Civil Rights era. Include 5 categories of questions with 5 questions in each category. Write your questions and answers on index cards. (More Difficult)
7. Research Martin Luther King, Jr. Find out how he dealt with and communicated to the American people about the injustices of racial prejudice. Do you think his methods would be effective today? Write a three page **position paper** explaining your point of view. (Most Difficult)	8. Find out about the Ku Klux Klan, the Niagara Movement, the NAACP and the National Urban League. Write an **essay** about the effects each had on the civil rights movement and how they affected and responded to each other. (Most Difficult)	9. Read a fiction book set during the Civil Rights era. Create a **Power Point presentation** summarizing the book. Include plot, characters, setting and theme. End your presentation by evaluating the impact of the civil rights movement on the characters in the book. (Most Difficult)

I/we chose activities # _____, #_____, and #_____.

Name _____   Due dates _____, _____, _____

World War II Tic-Tac-Toe
Student Choice Activities

Standard/Objective: Analyze America's participation in World War II

1. Write a **poem** about the roles and sacrifices of individual American soldiers during World War II. Include the special fighting forces in your poem.	2. Make a **concept map** outlining Roosevelt's foreign policy during World War II.	3. Make **collage** showing U.S. and Allied strategies during World War II. Use written facts, maps and pictures. Include Midway, Normandy, Iwo Jima, the Battle of the Bulge and at least two other events or battles.
4. Organize and lead a **Quiz Bowl** on the major developments in aviation, weaponry, medicine and communication during World War II.	5. **(Required Activity)** Do required reading and **answer questions** from textbook on World War II. Draw two **maps** showing countries and major battles in Europe/Africa and in Asia and the Pacific during World War II.	6. Write a **position paper** on the decision to drop the Atomic bomb on Hiroshima and Nagasaki and the consequences of this decision.
7. Write and direct a 10-15 minute **one-act play** depicting the impact of an event on the home front during World War II. This choice will be done as a group and performed for the class.	8. Make a five-minute **multi-media presentation** showing the effects of the Marshall Plan in Europe and how a rebuilt Europe affected the American economy.	9. Research the origin and causes of America's involvement in World War II. Give a 5 minute **oral report** that includes maps, a PowerPoint presentation and/or other visuals.

I/we chose activities # _____, #_____, and #_____.

Name _____ Due dates _____, _____, _____

Reproducible

How to Write Tic-Tac-Toe Student Activities

Tic-Tac-Toe activities are user-friendly and easy to write. Use this format for any grade level, subject or content. Follow the steps below to write your own.

____1. Decide on a major theme or topic for the student activities. This may be in conjunction with a certain unit of study or it may be generic, such as a spelling, writing or vocabulary Tic-Tac-Toe that could be used for several weeks or the entire school year.

____2. Look at your state standards in one or more subject areas to give you a focus for the activities you will write.

____3. List the topic and standards at the top of the Tic-Tac-Toe form.

____4. Start writing as many activities as you can think of that correlate with the standards and/or topic. Write each activity on separate small Post-it™ note.

____5. Place the Post-it™ notes with the activities on a blank Tic-Tac-Toe form in any order. You will find a blank form on the next page of this book and on the CD.

____6. Decide how you will set up the student choices. Move the Post-it™ notes around until you get the activities in appropriate positions so that no matter which way students choose, they will be doing the variety of activities you desire.

____7. When you have all activities in the desired order, write or type them onto a Tic-Tac-Toe form.

____8. If you develop a Tic-Tac-Toe and decide some of the activities in it are too difficult or too easy for some of your students, substitute a more appropriate activity or activities as needed. Many times you will only need to change one or two activities out of the nine to make a more difficult or less difficult version of the Tic-Tac-Toe. You could end up with tiered Tic-Tac-Toes, all of which focus on the same topic but with slightly different activities.

Note: See Chapter 7 on Differentiated Assessment to learn how to write Tic-Tac-Toe assessments.

_____**Tic-Tac-Toe Student Choice Activities**

Standards/Objectives: _____

_____

1.	2.	3.
4.	5.	6.
7.	8.	9.

I/we chose activities # _____, #_____, and #_____.

Name _____ Due dates _____, _____, _____

Reproducible

Helpful Hints
Using Student Choice Activities (Tic-Tac-Toe and ILP™)

All

- Differentiation means that sometimes students will be doing different products or activities in your class. Not every student needs to do every activity or do the same thing at the same time.

- Unless the activity is to be done at home, make sure you have all the materials (or require students to bring them to class) for students to create a product before offering it as a choice.

- Check to see that you have choices that challenge gifted and other high ability students. You can limit choices so that the gifted students are not allowed to pick the easiest option.

- Make sure you have choices that struggling students, English Language Learners or special needs students can do successfully.

- Choices must be standards-based. Standards from several subject areas can be combined within student choice activities.

K-3

- Introduce each product / performance in a whole group setting and have all students learn how to make or do it before offering it as an individual student choice.

- Choices can be indicated by pictures as well as words for students who can't read yet.

- Learning centers or stations are a good way to organize student choice activities for young students. Remember that in a differentiated classroom, every student does not have to go to every center.

- Use a bulletin board to show student choices.

- Limit the number of choices. Four choices rather than eight or nine are often better for young students.

Secondary

- Correlate due dates for major projects in each subject so students are not overwhelmed by too many big assignments that are due at the same time.

- Decide which of the student choice activities should be done at home and which you will give class time for students to work on.

Tiered Lessons or Units

Tiered lessons or units are multiple versions of assignments and activities that permit students to work at their appropriate level. They allow students to build on prior knowledge and skills. The unit objectives and standards being worked on are the same or similar for all students but are reached in different ways.

Tiered lessons are generally used with mixed ability classes. They give teachers a way to differentiate curriculum so that the levels are appropriate for different types of students without being too easy and boring for some or too difficult for others. In a classroom with no differentiation, the needs of both higher and lower level students are not met. Struggling students worry about being a failure or looking 'dumb', while high ability students often become unmotivated and never develop the study skills or work habits they need. Tiering is a differentiation strategy that addresses both of these concerns.

A tiered *lesson* is usually taught in one or two days. A tiered *unit* usually takes a week or two. Thus, the amount of time working in a tiered format is up to you. Whether it is a tiered lesson or unit, the planning format remains the same:

* List of objectives and standard

* Whole class activities

* Leveled activities (Levels 1, 2, and 3)

* Whole class culminating activities

The same planning steps are followed for a one or two day tiered lesson or unit of any length. Sometimes the culminating activities will lead into new whole class activities and the cycle will continue.

As much as is possible, make the leveled activities similar and parallel to one another. For example, when Level 1 students are doing a writing assignment, Levels 2 and 3 should be writing as well, just doing it in a more challenging way. Higher level work is not simply MORE work. It doesn't mean lower level kids write three sentences and higher level students write ten sentences.

A key to developing higher level work is to give students assignments with more depth (exploring an area of the topic in a more intense and profound way) and more complexity (exploring more aspects of the topic).

Using Bloom's Taxonomy is a good way to get ideas for tiering lessons and activities for students. Knowledge and Comprehension activities (Bloom's Levels 1 and 2) are often appropriate for Level 1 in a tiered lesson. Application, Analysis, Synthesis and Evaluation activities (Bloom's Levels 3-6) usually work well for Levels 2 and 3.

See *Bloom's and Beyond* (Pieces of Learning, publisher) for more information and ideas about Bloom's Taxonomy.

Levels for Tiering

For most tiered lessons, Level 1 is below grade level, Level 2 is at grade level and Level 3 is above grade level. Students are not necessarily in the same level for every activity. Find the best level for each student to meet the learning objectives and outcomes of the lesson or unit.

Teachers usually assign each student a level based on their own best judgment or on the basis of some type of pre-assessment or skills inventory.

These assessments can be formal in nature, such as a pretest, or can be more informal such as

- an observation of students

- a skills checklist

- a brainstorming activity

- class discussion.

You may also want to use KWL charts or webs that students fill in to show what they know about a certain topic.

Sometimes it is wise to give students a choice of two levels out of the three. You might want to have Level 1 and Level 2 activities on one sheet of paper (perhaps color coded, for example yellow) and Level 2 and Level 3 activities on another sheet of paper (perhaps color coded, for example blue). Give some students the yellow paper and others the blue. In theory all students could choose Level 2, but with this limited choice most should pick their most appropriate level.

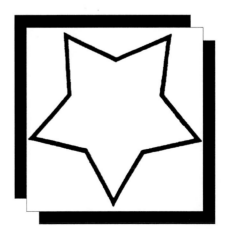

Tiered Lesson Plan: Unit Planning Form
Money in Different Countries

Objectives or Standards

1. To learn about money and prices in different countries
2. To understand how to convert money from one currency to another
3. To understand how to write a newspaper or magazine ad
4. To research information from print and non-print media

Whole Class Activities

1. Read text or an article supplied by the teacher about money around the world. Answer written questions and discuss as a whole class.
2. Demonstrate and have students practice converting money from U.S. dollars to another currency and vice-versa.
3. Show pictures or actual examples of money from a variety of different countries.

Assessment

1. Questions answered accurately and completely.

2. Practice converting several currencies.

Level 1 Activities

1. Choose one country. Find out the name of the currency, what it looks like and what it is worth. Take notes on what you find and illustrate or cut and paste a picture of the currency.

2. Choose 10 items you would like to purchase. Find out how much each costs in U.S. dollars. Convert each price to the currency of your chosen country.

3. Design an illustrated newspaper or magazine ad with your 10 chosen items and their prices in the currency of your country. Put the name of the country somewhere on your ad.

Assessment

1. Accurate for country chosen
   Neat illustrations of currency

2. Has ten items.
   Currency conversion is accurate

3. Neat with correct spelling
   Correct prices for each item
   Currency is named correctly in ad
   Has name of country
   Visually appealing ad

Level 2 Activities

1. Choose two different countries on different continents. Find out the name of the currency for each, what it looks like and what it is worth. Take notes and illustrate or cut and paste a picture of each type of currency.
2. Choose 10 items you would like to purchase. Find out how much each would cost in your two different countries. Convert their prices to U.S. dollars.
3. Design an illustrated newspaper or magazine ad for the country where you could buy these 10 items for the least amount of cost. Put the prices of the items in U.S. dollars and in the foreign country's currency. Put the name of your country somewhere in the ad

Assessment

1. Accurate for countries chosen
   Neat illustrations of currencies

2. Has ten items.
   Currency conversions are accurate for both countries.

3. Neat with correct spelling
   Prices are accurate and ones chosen are the least costly.
   Prices are in U.S. dollars and in the foreign currency.
   Has name of country
   Visually appealing ad

Level 3 Activities

1. Choose two different countries, one 'First World' wealthy country and one 'Third World' impoverished country. Find out the name of the currency for each, what it looks like and what it is worth. Take notes and illustrate or cut and paste pictures of each type of currency.
2. Choose 10 items you would like to purchase. Find out how much each would cost in your two different countries. Convert their prices to U.S. dollars. Write a paragraph evaluating the differences you see and the reasons for these differences. If there are some items that cannot be purchased in one of your countries, explain why.
3. Design a newspaper or magazine ad showing the 10 items, the prices in each currency, plus the cost of each in U.S. dollars. Put the names of each country beside the corresponding prices.

Assessment

1. Accurate for countries chosen
   Have one 'First World' and one 'Third World' country
   Neat illustrations of currencies

2. Has ten items.
   Currency conversions are accurate for both countries.
   Differences are noted and reasons given.
   Correct spelling, punctuation and grammar

3. Neat with correct spelling
   Prices are accurate
   Shows prices in all three currencies.
   Names of countries are beside each price.
   Visually appealing ad.

Whole Class Activities

1. In heterogeneous groups, share research on currencies in chosen countries. Each group member will show and explain his/her ad to the group.
2. Each group will make a poster of "Money Around the World". Currencies from group members' countries will be displayed and labeled on the poster.
3. Each group will present their poster to the class along with conclusions they have made about money/currencies throughout the world. Each group should have at least five conclusions.

Assessment

1. All group members listening to one another and sharing their work.

2. Follows Poster Criteria Card
   Currencies from each group member are on the poster.
   Currencies are labeled correctly.

3. Follows Oral Report Criteria Card.
   Has five conclusions about money throughout the world.

Tiered Activities

Writing Tiered Lessons or Units

Writing tiered lessons and units can be challenging. Below are some steps to guide your planning. Use the blank Tiered Lesson form on the next page to write your own Tiered Lessons or Unit.

1. Establish which standards, objectives, knowledge or skills all students need to know at the end of this lesson or unit. Use your state's standards documents to guide you.

2. Think about activities you have done with students in the past to reach these standards or objectives. Brainstorm with other teachers and use your resources to get other ideas. Use the Initial Planning Form to make a list of activities. Write each activity on the first line for each item on the form.

3. Decide which are appropriate learning activities for all students. These will become your whole class activities. Label these **WC**.

4. Some of the activities on your list will most likely be easier than others. Label the level or tier you think each activity might be. Consider your class and decide on how many levels you need to have. I usually have two or three levels.

5. Think about ways to expand or extend the easier activities so they will be challenging for higher ability students, and ways to simplify the more difficult activities so that your struggling students can do them successfully.

6. Look carefully at your list of activities. Many times you will have more activities than you could possibly do given the amount of time you have for the unit. Decide which activities are essential and which could be eliminated if necessary. You may want to save a couple of activities to use as anchoring activities with students at any level who finish their work before others.

7. Check again to make sure all activities will lead to students learning the standards and objectives.

8. Make certain that activities at all levels are engaging and interesting. Nothing discourages achievement faster than students thinking that the other group is the one with the fun, interesting or enjoyable activity while the learning activity they have been assigned is not.

9. Write your unit or lesson plan using the Tiered Lesson Plan format.

10. Check to see that the activities at one level are parallel to the ones done at another level. For example, are all students creating a visual or are all students doing research? Tiered lessons are easiest to implement when activities at all levels are similar to one another.

11. Plan daily lessons based on your tiered lesson or unit plan.

12. As you would with any lesson or unit, gather supplies and resources needed to do the activities.

Note: *The Tiered Lesson Plan format includes assessments for each of the tiered activities. We will discuss assessment more fully in the next chapter.*

Initial Planning Form for a Tiered Unit

Theme or Topic:_____

Standards/Benchmarks:_____
_____
_____
_____

Possible Student Activities   **Levels of Difficulty**

1. _____   _____

   _____   _____

   _____   _____

2. _____   _____

   _____   _____

   _____   _____

3. _____   _____

   _____   _____

   _____   _____

4. _____   _____

   _____   _____

   _____   _____

5. _____   _____

   _____   _____

   _____   _____

6. _____   _____

   _____   _____

   _____   _____

Tiered Lesson Plan: Unit Planning Form

_____

Objectives
or
Standards

1.

2.

3.

4.

Whole Class Activities

Assessment

Level 1 Activities

Assessment

Level 2 Activities   Assessment

Level 3 Activities   Assessment

Whole Class Culminating Activities   Assessment

Grading Tiered Assignments

Grading tiered assignments often produces the most concern when teachers decide to implement this strategy. The problem seems to be how to set up the points for each level. Experts in the field of differentiation have differing opinions about grading. I believe this is because as a profession, educators have not come to any consensus about what grades actually mean. Grading is not standardized from school to school, grade level to grade level or even teacher to teacher!

There are several options for grading tiered lessons. I have listed three in the next column. There is no inherent correct or incorrect way to grade student work in a tiered unit or lesson. I think it is essential for teachers within a school (or at least within a grade level) to come to consensus about how all of them will do grading. Use the Reflection Questions on the next page to guide your thinking on tiering and grading.

Below are some possible ways to handle the grading dilemma:

1. Have activities at all levels equal the same number of points. The idea here is that if students are working at their appropriate level, they should be graded according to how well they have done at that level and not in comparison to other students.

2. Give more points to students who attempt the higher level tasks. For example, a Level 1 activity might be worth a total of 85 points while a Level 3 activity might be worth 100 points.

3. Decide which level represents grade level work and have that level worth 100 points. Students working at a lower level would receive less points and those working at a higher level could receive bonus or additional points.

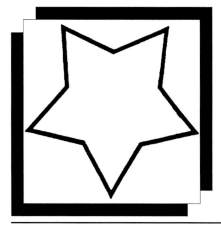

Teacher Reflection Questions
Tiered Lessons and Units

1. Have you ever done a tiered lesson or unit with you students? If so, share what happened. What were the pluses and minuses? If not, why not?

2. What ideas do you have for managing students when they are doing different assignments?

3. What are your thoughts about assessing and grading tiered activities?

4. What concerns do you have about using tiered lessons in your classroom?

5. What subject areas or units of work do you think would be most successful for using tiered lessons?

6. What is you plan of action for using tiered lessons in the future?

Helpful Hints for Writing and Using Tiered Activities

- For K-1 students, think of tiers as 'I can't read or write yet'; 'I can read but I can't write yet'; and 'I can read and write'. Design activities for the three tiers or levels accordingly.

- For most tiered lessons, Level 1 is below grade level, Level 2 is at grade level and Level 3 is above grade level.

- Color code tiered activities for easy organization and grouping of students.

- Tiered activities can be done in groups or individually depending on what the activity is.

- It is easiest to tier lessons and units when the activities done at each level are parallel to one another.

- Try to make each level's activities ones that will take the same amount of time. Have another activity ready to go for anyone who finishes early.

- Use tiered learning centers or stations with activities at different levels of difficulty at each center. (A good resource is *Tiered Activities for Learning Centers* published by Pieces of Learning.)

- Use formal pretests but also use your own judgment as to what level is the right one for each student.

- Establish a grade level or school wide policy for grading tiered assignments. This makes it much easier for an individual teacher to defend the way he or she is grading.

Encounter Lessons

Encounter lessons are open-ended lessons that encourage good listening skills, stimulate creativity and higher level thinking, and provide motivation for all students. They are often used at the beginning of a unit of study. Encounter lessons help the teacher to personalize the topic for the students and open up discussion in a non-threatening way. Differentiation in Encounter Lessons comes from the extenders which range in difficulty and can be chosen or assigned according to ability or interest.

Excluding the extenders, these lessons usually last from 20-30 minutes and are best done in small groups of 5 students per group. Heterogeneous groups usually work well in this situation. Encounter lessons have open-ended questions that ask the student to pretend he or she is an object, a place or a famous person and to respond to the question accordingly.

There are five Leading Questions in an Encounter Lesson. Each student in the group answers one question in 'round robin' fashion. The answer to the second question is based upon what was said in answer to the first question. Therefore, Encounter Lessons are excellent for building listening skills. Appoint a facilitator for each group to keep the activity focused and moving along.

Another way to use the Encounter Lesson is to have each student answer all of the questions. Sometimes this is done in written form first and then shared in pairs or trios.

A different approach is to use the Encounter Lesson format is for review at the end of a unit of work. In this case, you would eliminate the Differentiated Extenders. This is a motivational and creative way to review a unit of study!

On the next several pages you will find:

➢ Directions for structuring and writing Encounter Lessons

➢ A Greek Mythology Encounter Lesson with Differentiated Extenders

➢ A blank Encounter Lesson form for writing your own

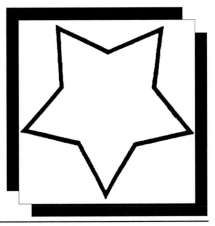

Structuring and Writing an Encounter Lesson

Title:
The title should reflect the major theme or focus of the lesson.

Boundary Breaker:
This is an easily answered non-threatening question which usually reveals some thing about each student's feelings or opinions. If a student does not want to answer a Boundary Breaker, he or she can say *"pass."* After everyone else has answered, the group facilitator will return to anyone who has said *"pass"* to see if they would now like to answer. If they still do not want to give an answer, they say "'pass, pass."

Setting the Stage:
This sets the scene for the questions. The group facilitator sets the stage, telling the group what person, place or object each person needs to pretend to be and what the scenario for the lesson is.

Leading Questions:

1. This is the description question. In answering this question, the person should describe something.

2. This question asks for a reason and usually begins with the word 'Why'.

3. This is the storytelling question. In answering this question, the person should tell a story or relate an imaginary incident that has happened.

4. This is the motto, slogan or message question. The answer to this question should be short – usually 10 words or less.

5. The answer to this question shows some kind of change or transformation. It may be phrased as a 'What would happen if?' question, an 'imagine' question, or a question that reflects a new point of view.

Standards/Objectives:
Listed here are the grade level standards that will be addressed by the Extenders.

Differentiated Extenders:
The extenders are the activities in the unit of work itself. There is no limit to the num-ber of extenders an Encounter Lesson may have. Sometimes these are student choice activities and other times they are required for everyone or are chosen by the teacher for individual students. The extenders could take anywhere from one or two days to several weeks to complete, depending upon how many each student has to do and how extensive they are.

Greek Mythology Encounter Lesson

Title:
Mt. Olympus – Home of the Gods

Boundary Breaker:
Describe the most beautiful scene in nature that you have ever seen.

Setting the Stage:
You are Mt. Olympus, home of the Greek gods and goddesses. You've been around since the dawn of time! You wish you could retire and make all of the gods and goddesses go live somewhere else. Your life is pretty hectic with all of them living on you.

Leading Questions:

1. Describe what your life was like before you were inhabited by the Greek gods and goddesses.

2. You are famous and eternal! Why would you want to retire anyway?

3. Tell a story about what happened to one of the gods or goddesses who is living on you.

4. If you sold a bumper sticker on the top of Mt. Olympus, what would it say?

5. Imagine the all powerful Zeus granting you, Mt. Olympus, one special wish. This wish could change your life. What would you wish for and why?

Standards/Objectives:

1. Gain an understanding of the enormous impact and influence Greek mythology has made on western literature and thought.

2. Read and analyze myths representing diverse backgrounds, traditions and points of view.

3. Understand the literary elements (plot, characterization, setting, mood, point of view) in Greek myths.

4. Organize, write and present ideas.

Differentiated Extenders for the Greek Mythology Unit:

1. Design a series of 5 picture postcards from Mt. Olympus. The pictures should show the geography of Mt. Olympus or a story about a god or goddess who lives there. On the other side of each postcard, write a message explaining the picture.

2. Choose a Greek myth. Research sources to find a similar myth from another culture. Write a paper comparing and contrasting the two myths.

3. Choose a Greek god or goddess. Make a chart listing his or her character traits and the character traits of a famous person of today. Include both strengths and weaknesses and give examples for each trait.

4. Update a Greek myth to fit modern times. Rewrite the myth as a one-act play, using the attitudes, language and setting of today. Perform for the class. (At least 3 people must make this choice and must work together.)

5. Select an act of nature. Explain it by writing a myth in the style of a Greek myth.

6. Choose your favorite Greek god or goddess. Create a series of 10 interview questions and write what you think his or her answers would be. Stay in character for the god or goddess you have chosen.

7. Write a job description for Hades, the god of the Underworld.

8. Retell any Greek myth using a comic strip. You must have at least 10 frames.

9. Make a model of Mount Olympus. Include a card or labels of important facts.

10. Compare and contrast the journeys of Jason and the Argonauts with Odysseus and his men.

Encounter Lesson Form

Title:

Boundary Breaker:

Setting the Stage:

Leading Questions:

1.

2.

3.

4.

5.

Standards/Objectives:

Differentiated Extenders:

To Summarize . . .
Formats for Writing Differentiated Lessons and Units

➤ Writing differentiated lessons and units takes careful planning and preparation.

➤ There are several practical, easy-to-use planning formats to help you plan for differentiated instruction in your classroom.

➤ Use the ILP™ format to structure a unit with both *Teacher Required* and *Student Choice* activities.

➤ Number student choices on both the ILP™ and the Tic-Tac-Toe. Keep track of which activities students choose by using the numbered Activity Chart.

➤ Use the Tic-Tac-Toe format to give students choices of three learning activities within a unit of work. This format can also be used for generic assignments that are repeated week after week such as spelling, vocabulary, writing prompts, etc.

➤ There are a number of ways to set up student choices on the Tic-Tac-Toe.

➤ Tiered lessons and units are best used in mixed-ability classes where all students work toward the same standards at different levels of readiness or ability.

➤ Come to consensus with your colleagues about how grading will be handled in a differentiated classroom. There are several different approaches, all of which work better when there is agreement about how to do it within a school, department or grade level.

➤ Encounter Lessons encourage creative thinking and provide motivation for students. Use these at the beginning of a unit with the Differentiated Extenders making up the work of the unit. You can also use an Encounter Lesson (without the Extenders) to review at the end of a unit of work.

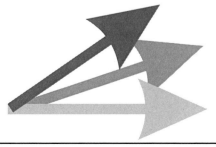

Differentiated Assessment

Characteristics

Three types of assessments

Developing assessment criteria

Rubrics

Criteria Cards

Mini-rubrics

Tiered tests and quizzes

Grading

Characteristics of Assessment in the Differentiated Classroom

It seems obvious that if teachers differentiate their instruction, they will also have to differentiate assessment. Students who do different learning activities need to be assessed in different ways. This can be a particularly difficult concept when so much assessment is now standardized.

Assessment most certainly plays a crucial role in differentiated instruction. Without it we cannot pinpoint what our students already know or what they need to learn. We cannot target specific skills for instruction or flexibly group our students. We cannot see progress and growth over time. Assessment has a vital function in all of these.

In general, the purpose of assessment in a differentiated classroom is to show students' individual growth and improvement and to target what each student can and cannot do. To accomplish these goals, assessments may include open-ended tasks where students can demonstrate their knowledge and show higher levels of thinking in applying this knowledge to new problems or situations.

Differentiated assessment also means assessing student products and performances in different ways, using rubrics, checklists, learning logs, self assessment, observations etc. instead of one standardized assessment for all students.

A simple checklist may be all that is needed for some products and performances. You may want to keep these in a portfolio in order to show growth and effort over time. You can also differentiate assessment by using more complex rubrics that list specific criteria and define levels of competence and excellence.

Differentiated products and performances usually cover many different standards; therefore they can be more difficult and complex to score. Using rubrics, criteria cards, mini-rubrics and checklists helps teachers score student work and grade more accurately and fairly.

Teachers have a number concerns about how they should assess students in the differentiated classroom, especially when it comes to grading. If all students are not doing the same work or turning in the same assignments, the argument goes, how can we grade our students fairly?

In this chapter, we will look at assessment as it relates to differentiated instruction. We will see how to establish assessment criteria and how to write rubrics. We will look at approaches for giving students feedback and examine ways to grade differentiated products and performances.

Three Types of Assessments
Helpful in Differentiating Instruction

There are three major types of assessments that can be used in the differentiated classroom. To be useful, all three should be aligned with curricular and instructional objectives and with state standards. The three types are:

➤ Pre-assessments
➤ Formative assessments
➤ Summative assessments

Most rubrics or checklists can be used as formative assessments, summative assessments or both. Pre-assessment is usually done via a pretest, student observation, a checklist or some other evidence of past work and knowledge. Let's look more closely at these three types of assessment.

Pre-assessment is...

Any method, strategy or process used to determine a student's current level of readiness, knowledge or interest in order to plan for appropriate instruction.

➤ Provides data and information to show the learning levels of each student before planning instruction. This helps in understanding each student's needs and the nature of learning differences between various students in a given classroom.

➤ Helps teachers determine learning options for students functioning at different levels or with different sets of knowledge and skills.

➤ Allows students to demonstrate mastery or to show where remediation might be needed before instruction begins.

➤ Makes it easier for students to build on what they already know.

Formative Assessment is...

The process of accumulating information about a student's progress on a regular basis as he or she is working. This helps in making ongoing instructional decisions for a particular student or group of students during a unit of work.

Using formative assessment, teachers can change, modify, extend or make adjustments in the instructional activities students are doing. It is assessment for learning rather than assessment of learning.

➤ Alerts the teacher early on about student misconceptions or lack of understanding about what is being studied.

➤ Provides regular feedback to students.

➤ Supplies evidence of progress in learning over time.

> Gives students a chance to correct their mistakes and learn from them before the final project or learning activity is turned in.

> Offers current information about the progress students are making while working on an individual product or performance.

> Lists guidelines and criteria for success students can refer to and use as they are doing their work.

A summary of more that 250 research studies found that formative assessment contributes more to improving student achievement than any other school-based factor. It also found that while formative assessment benefits all students, it benefits low achievers even more than high achievers. (Black & Wiliam, 1998.)

Summative Assessment is...

A means to determine a student's mastery of information, knowledge, skills, concepts, etc. after the unit or learning activity has been completed. The name originates with the idea that these assessments summarize the learning that has taken place.

> Should parallel the formative assessments used during the learning process and should usually use the same assessment instruments.

> May determine a report card grade or score.

> Can be the basis for making a final decision about a student.

> Should align with instructional/curricular objectives, standards and benchmarks.

> May be a form of alternative assessment; doesn't always have to be a test.

Can be high stakes such as a standardized test or report card that determines promotion to the next grade level or entry into a certain college.

Rubrics, checklists, criteria cards, learning logs, portfolios, rating scales, peer reviews, self-editing and a host of other strategies can be used as both formative and summative assessments. How they are used is the distinguishing factor in whether they are formative or summative.

Teacher Reflection Questions
Three Types of Assessment

1. Which of these three types of assessment do you use the most? Why?

2. Give examples of ways pre-assessments can be helpful and useful in the classroom.

3. How and why do formative assessments help in raising student achievement? What has been your experience in using them?

4. Do you think summative assessments are overly emphasized in schools? Why or why not?

Developing Assessment Criteria

Nearly all student projects, products and performances could be assessed in a multitude of different ways. Because we are in standards-based educational systems, looking at the standards is the place to start when developing assessment criteria. Considering the standards and then determining the significant learning outcomes for each piece of student work is the first step.

Simply stated in question form, you should ask yourself,

- "Why am I having my students do this work or this project?"
  The answer to that question is the major learning outcome. The next question should be,
- "What standards will they be working on?"
  Finally, you should ask yourself,
- "Can I picture what the finished product will look like?"

If you can, developing assessment criteria is merely putting that mental picture into words. On the other hand, if you say, "I don't know what it will look like but I'll know a good one when I see it", the chances are that you won't be able to write clear assessment criteria!

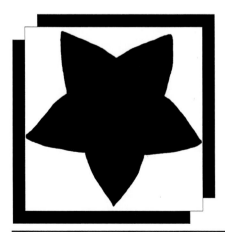

Assessment criteria provide a focus and direction for the student and give the teacher a concrete way to assess what each student does. Be clear on what learning outcomes you want your students to achieve. This is a good way to begin thinking about assessment criteria. High-quality assessment criteria should reflect advanced levels in self-directed learning, thinking, research and communication.

After identifying the standards and establishing the learning outcomes, the next step is to list the criteria. Brainstorm all possible criteria you might want to consider in assessing the stated learning outcomes. Make sure your criteria correspond to the standards and learning outcomes you have identified.

If you have an exceptionally long list of criteria, it may be necessary to pare it down or to combine two or more of your criteria into one item. I often list ten or twelve criteria but then identify four or five of the most important ones. I think having too many assessment criteria for a product or performance causes students to lose focus and feel overwhelmed. On the other hand, a limited number of criteria targets the most important items and seem more doable to the student.

This listing of standards, learning outcomes and specific criteria provides the beginning point for constructing a rubric. In the next portion of this chapter, we will examine both complex rubrics and mini-rubrics and see how to construct and use each.

Rubrics: Tools for Differentiated Assessment

Rubrics are a type of specific directions or guidelines for student work. They identify criteria that serve as indicators to students as to what is most important in a project or performance. Most complex rubrics also contain some type of rating scale so that various levels of student performance can be indicated.

Good rubrics help us evaluate all types of products and performances more fairly since they require us to be more precise about what our expectations and criteria for assessment are. With rubrics, students and teachers alike understand exactly how student work is evaluated. The criteria are most definitely not a secret! Being clear about them gives students an understanding of the meaning behind their grade or final assessment.

Teachers use specific criteria on the rubric to guide them in grading and evaluating student products and performances. Looking at the same criteria gives students feedback on their work. In this way, they have useful information about they have done and about their progress as learners. Many students are encouraged to explore topics in more depth based on the feedback from rubrics, especially when these are used as formative assessments.

Rubrics can be developed by the teacher or in conjunction with the students themselves. Developing a rubric together is a great way to show students exactly how they will be assessed. It helps them understand more fully both the elements of an excellent project or piece of work and how it will be graded. This should never be a mystery!

A typical complex rubric:

➤ Contains a scale of possible points or categories to be assigned for varying degrees of mastery or quality.
➤ States the different traits or criteria used to evaluate the product or performance.
➤ Provides pointers or descriptors for assessing each of the criteria. These help in showing us the right place on the scoring scale to which a particular student's work corresponds.

There are no rules about how many criteria you need to have in a rubric or how many levels need to be indicated. In general, I like to have no more than four or five levels. The number of criteria should be no more than five or six. The more levels and the more criteria, the more cumbersome the rubric becomes. From a practical standpoint, most students stop reading rubrics or directions when they are too complex or wordy.

In addition, extremely long rubrics are difficult for teachers to use. If the purpose of a rubric is to give feedback to the student or to help the teacher accurately and fairly score or grade a piece of student work, we want the process to be as simple and understandable as possible!

As indicated above, rubrics usually have a scoring scale. I often use a scale with five levels. Level 4 indicates grade level mastery and Level 5 is an extension level.

My five levels of a rubric scale are:

1 = You attempted the project/performance and turned something in, but it falls far short of expected quality.

2 = Your product/performance needs more work, additional elements or more thought.

3 = Your product/performance needs minor corrections, changes or additions, but for the most part it is OK.

4 = Your product/performance is complete and done well.

5 = You have gone above and beyond the requirements and expectations for this product/performance. You have extended learning beyond the assignment's requirements, show higher level thinking and/or creativity and a unique approach to the task. (Extension level)

In this scale, Level 5 is especially important for gifted and high achieving students. Many times these students can get A's on assignments without putting forth much effort or thought. They need rubrics that show ways to extend their work beyond the expected grade level norm. This encourages them to work toward excellence instead of mediocrity. It also allows them to build on what they already know and progress independently at their own rate of speed.

Therefore, the top level in any rubric should be a way to show that a student has gone above and beyond the assigned work or expectations. This is particularly important because we do not want them to stop learning once they have reached the minimum expectation for a project or performance! Instead, we must continue to challenge them and to indicate this within the rubric itself.

Some rubrics are written with the highest number of the scale first. I prefer to begin with the lowest acceptable level on the scale and go from there. This is because I want the students to see a progression of learning as they read each line of the rubric. Level 1 on the rubric scale means little more than the student turned something in! Each subsequent level indicates further progression in accomplishing the standards or learning outcomes for the project.

The scale in any rubric can be translated into points for grading student work. Teachers have different ideas about exactly how many points should be awarded for each level on a rubric. I like the first level on the rubric to indicate a minimal passing score. I do not accept student work that is below that level. Therefore, a student who scored all 1's on a rubric should score approximately 60 points.

On page 151 is a blank rubric form with suggested points for each level. Using these points:

All criteria at Level 1 = 60 points total

All criteria at Level 2 = 72 points total

All criteria at Level 3 = 84 points total

All criteria at Level 4 = 96 points total

One or more at Level 5 = 100+

On page 152 you will find a blank rubric form you can use to write your own rubrics.

Developing a Rubric:
An Example

One of the Extender Activities from the Encounter Lesson (page 138) is below. The standards and learning outcomes for this activity and a list of criteria for assessment are included. On the following page is a sample rubric used to assess this activity.

Activity:

Choose a Greek god or goddess. Make a chart listing his or her character traits and similar character traits of a famous person of today. Include both strengths and weaknesses and give examples for each trait.

Standards/Learning Outcomes:

• Show an understanding of how Greek mythology has made an impact on current thinking.

• Analyze character traits of a character a Greek myth.

• Organize, write and present ideas.

Assessment Criteria:

• Includes a Greek god or goddess and a famous person from today.

• Lists character traits and examples of each.

• Indicates strengths and weaknesses.

• Presents ideas clearly in chart form. (Chart criteria card*)

Note: Criteria cards are explained in the next section of this chapter.

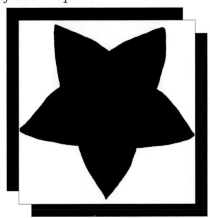

Rubric - <u>Chart of Character Traits: Greek God or Goddess and Famous Person Today</u>

NAME: DATE:

Standards/Outcomes:
1. Show understanding of how Greek mythology has made an impact on current thinking.
2. *Analyze* character traits of a character in a Greek myth.
3. Organize, write, and present ideas.

CRITERIA	1	2	3	4	5 Extension	Points
Identifies Greek god/goddess and famous person of today and lists similar character traits.	Identifies only god or goddess but not famous person. 1-2 character traits.	Identifies god/goddess and famous person and 1-2 character traits.	Identifies god/goddess and famous person and 3-4 character traits.	Identifies god/goddess and famous person and 5 or more character traits.	Everything in #4 PLUS identifies unusual/unique traits that both have.	
Gives examples of each trait for both the Greek god/goddess and the famous person of today.	Has 1-2 examples for famous person or the god/goddess but not both.	Has 1-2 examples for famous person and the god/goddess.	Has 3-4 examples for famous person and the god/goddess.	Examples for each of the 5 or more traits for god/goddess and for famous person.	Gives little known examples; links traits of both in uncommon ways.	
Indicates which traits are strengths and which are weaknesses.	Indicates strengths or weaknesses for 1-2 traits but doesn't explain why.	Indicates strengths or weaknesses for 1-2 traits and explains why.	Indicates strengths or weaknesses for 3-4 traits and explains why.	Explains each of the 5 or more traits as a strength or weakness and indicates why.	Explains each of the 5 or more traits as both a strength and a weakness and indicates why.	
Follows Chart criteria card.	Has 1 item on criteria card.	Has 2 items on criteria card.	Has 3 items on criteria card.	Has all 4 items on criteria card.	Visually striking chart; extremely detailed and understandable.	
				Grade		**Total points**

© Pieces of Learning

RUBRIC FOR _____

NAME: _____

DATE: _____

This shows one way to embed points into a rubric with five levels and four criteria. Level 4 is the grade level standard. Level 5 is an extension beyond the grade level expectation. Level 1 is minimally acceptable work.

CRITERIA	1 15 points each	2 18 points each	3 21 points each	4 24 points each	5 Extension 25-28 each
Points	All 1's = 60%	All 2's = 72%	All 3's = 84%	All 4's = 96%	Can earn 100% or higher
Total points				**Grade**	

RUBRIC FOR _____

NAME:

DATE:

Standards/Outcomes:

CRITERIA	1	2	3	4	5 Extension
			Points		
			Total points	Grade	

© Pieces of Learning

Product and Process Criteria Cards

Sometimes you may have the same generic criteria for certain products, processes, or performances regardless of the specific academic content they cover. These are most likely processes you want the student to focus on at all times or products they do more than once. These may well be products and processes they do for several different teachers.

Examples of generic processes include certain writing conventions (grammar, mechanics and sentence structure) or a skill like research skills or organizational skills. It might even be classroom expectations such as turning in ones work on time. In addition, there are hundreds of products students can do. Look again at Chapter 5 for a listing of many of these included in each of the Learning Preference categories.

A great assessment short cut and time saver is to assess these products and processes by using Criteria Cards that students can draw on and refer to over and over again. These cards have short, easily understood lists of criteria (generally 4-5) that students can look at each time they use the same process or complete the same product. If all teachers at a given grade level in elementary school or throughout a team or department at the middle and high school level would use the same criteria cards, students would benefit greatly.

In addition, if we would start articulating student products and performances in the same way we do the rest of the curriculum, teachers at one grade level could pass along criteria cards to teachers at the next grade level. Wouldn't it be nice to know that all of the third graders who come to you on the first day of 4th grade have had experience making a brochure or creating a PowerPoint or developing a Venn diagram or designing a diorama? We almost never have such information, however, so we make assumptions about what our students know how to do. Many times we really don't know what their experience is. Criteria cards at different grade levels could definitely help with this!

On the next two pages you will see 20 criteria cards targeting a variety of student activities and products. They are in alphabetical order for easy reference. Many of them refer to student products and performances contained in the sample Individual Lesson Plan and Tic-Tac-Toes in Chapter 6. Use these as a starting point for differentiating assessments and then continue to write your own.

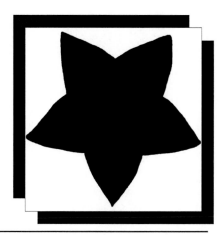

Criteria Cards

Product and Process Criteria Cards

Brochure
1. Highlights important points
2. Folded with information on each side
3. Neatly done
4. Visually appealing with pictures
5. Titles correctly spelled

Debate
1. Observes allotted time
2. States opinion clearly
3. Backs up opinion with evidence from reliable sources
4. Respectful of other side; no name calling

Chart
1. Has two or more sections divided by lines
2. Title and subtitles
3. Shows information clearly
4. Neat with correct spelling

Diagram
1. Items in logical and accurate order
2. Visually shows relationship between parts or ideas
3. Neat drawing and writing
4. Object or process drawn accurately

Class Participation
1. Shows good listening skills
2. Asks appropriate questions
3. Stays on the topic
4. Offers ideas and opinions

Group Work
1. Stays on topic
2. Listens to others in group
3. Sets group goals
4. Works to meet goals
5. Uses time wisely

Collage
1. Has a solid backing
2. Pictures/objects overlap
3. Title/labels spelled correctly
4. Visually attractive and neat
5. Pictures/objects relate to topic

Information Cube
1. Cube is sturdy and has six sides
2. Has required information on each side of cube.
3. Accurate information
4. Neat and visually attractive

Comic Strip
1. Frames in correct sequence
2. Tells a story through pictures and words
3. Neatly drawn
4. Is humorous

Log of Project Work
1. Has date for each day
2. At least two sentences about what was accomplished each day
3. Shows goals and plans for next day
4. Reflections and questions included

Map	**Poster**
1. Shows shapes of land and water 2. Correct scale 3. Places labeled and spelled correctly 4. Accurate information shown	1. On poster board 2. Legible, neat writing 3. Has visuals about topic 4. Has title and labels spelled correctly 5. Neat with white space
Model	**PowerPoint Presentation**
1. Accurate representation 2. Durable construction 3. Neatly done 4. 3-dimensional	1. At least 10 slides 2. Pictures and words are coordinated 3. Technology works correctly 4. Includes some animation 5. Well organized
Oral Presentation/Report	**Skit**
1. Clear speaking loud enough for all to hear 2. Good eye contact 3. Uses gestures and visuals 4. Correct timing	1. Realistic dialogue 2. Actions and words support plot 3. Script and acting are coordinated 4. Costumes and props help tell story
Poem	**Time Line**
1. Appropriate format 2. Has a poetic structure 3. Correct spelling and punctuation 4. Title 5. Relevant to subject	1. Title 2. Chronological order 3. Important events/dates included 4. Well-plotted time spans 5. Neat and legible
Position Paper	**Venn Diagram**
1. Shows knowledge of position 2. Evidence and resources to support position 3. Correct spelling, grammar and punctuation 4. Position is clear	1. Has two or more overlapping circles 2. Shows similarities and differences 3. Has title and conclusions 4. Neat and clear writing 5. Accurate

Product and Process Criteria Card: Write Your Own

Using Criteria Cards: Helpful Hints

All

- Share criteria cards between grade levels. It is helpful to know which products students have learned how to do at a previous grade level.

- Ask gifted and other high ability students what they could add to each criteria card to make their products show additional higher level thinking.

- Write criteria cards clearly but in a general way so that they can be used with any content or subject.

K-3

- Design product criteria cards with your students as you introduce each product.

- Make the language on the cards simple enough that is completely understandable to your students.

- Post each of the criteria on the wall of bulletin board for easy reference.

- You might want to color-code the cards according to categories such as Visual, Written, Hands-on, Speaking, etc.

- Make your criteria cards on half or full sheets of paper and include a picture of the product as well as the criteria for the product. *

* Note: A sample criteria card appropriate for K-3 students is on the next page. There is also a blank form for writing your own.

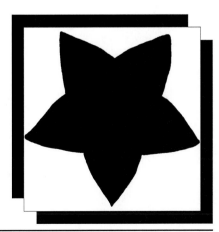

Diorama

➤ Is in an open box

➤ Has a colorful background

➤ Has 3-D objects in it

➤ Helps you show something you know about

Name of Product

➤

➤

➤

➤

➤

Reproducible © Pieces of Learning

Mini-Rubrics

Mini-rubrics are short lists of assessment criteria that can be used to guide students while they are working on products or performances. They are also used to grade completed student work.

Complex rubrics are a wonderful tool for evaluating student work and for encouraging excellence in learning. As much as I like them, however, I was puzzled about how to use rubrics when I began to explore the idea of giving students a number of differentiated choices to consider within a unit of work. I had been using both the ILP™ and Tic-Tac-Toes with students but found it difficult and time consuming to create complex rubrics for each of the student choice activities.

A workable solution for me has been to use mini-rubrics. In designing them, I eliminated the rows, columns and descriptors found in complex rubrics. By doing that, I gained the capability of including eight or nine mini-rubrics on one sheet of paper to correspond to the choice activities on an ILP™ or Tic-Tac-Toe.

Students read the mini-rubric for each activity before making a choice of which they want to work on. Extensions can be included in mini-rubrics and serve the same function in challenging high ability students as the extension column does in a complex rubric.

Because of the limited amount of space available to write each mini-rubric, criteria cards are particularly useful. As is appropriate, include a criteria card as one of the criteria listed on your mini-rubric. The remainder of the criteria should target the content and standards on which the activity focuses.

Mini-rubrics have a space for the number of possible points for the activity and spaces to indicate points or to check off each of the specific criteria. In my examples on pages 161 and 163, you will see these spaces. I have not indicated specific points because each teacher has his or her own point system to use. When you write your own mini-rubrics, however, indicate your points on them so your students will understand exactly how their work will be graded.

On the next four pages you will find:

➢ A mini-rubric used to assess the student choice activities in the ILP™ on Natural Disasters found on page 106
➢ A blank mini-rubric form to use with student choice activities in ILPs™
➢ A mini-rubric used to assess the student choice activities in the Tic-Tac-Toe on Fairy Tales found on page 115
➢ A blank mini-rubric form to use with Tic-Tac-Toe activities

Use the blank forms to write your own mini-rubrics.

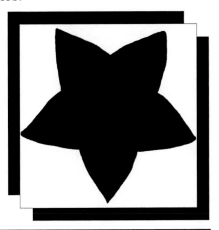

How to Write Mini-Rubrics

1. Look at the standards, benchmarks and learning outcomes for your unit. Keep these in mind as you write the mini-rubrics.

2. Note the product or performance that is required in each student activity. These are generally written in boldface and underlined on an ILP™ or Tic-Tac-Toe.

3. Write the name of each product or performance at the top of each numbered space on the mini-rubric.

4. Decide if you want to use a criteria card as part of your mini-rubric. If so, write: 'Follows _____ criteria card' on the first line of your mini-rubric. If you don't have a criteria card for a specific product, you might want to create one.

5. Write 2-4 more criteria in addition to the criteria card. These should specifically pinpoint the content. Sometimes you will almost repeat what the activity says.

6. Ask yourself: "Do these criteria define what I want from the students doing this activity?" If not, make your criteria more specific.

7. Include lines for points or checks beside each of the criteria you list.

8. Write a *Suggested Extension*. This should be an activity that will take the student to a higher level of thinking or will require additional research and study.

9. Decide how many points each activity is worth. Indicate this by writing 'Possible points = _____ (your points here)'

Assessment of Student Choices - Individual Lesson Plan- Natural Disasters

1. Venn Diagram (Visual)

- Follows Venn Diagram criteria card _____
- Accurate information about earthquakes & tsunamis _____
- Conclusions reflect on similarities and differences _____

Suggested extension: Make a Venn Diagram with 3 circles and include another type of natural disaster. _____

Possible points = _____

2. Map & Paragraph (Visual)

- Follows Map criteria card _____
- Hurricanes accurately plotted _____
- Paragraph clearly explains conclusions _____
- Conclusions are related to map information _____
- Correct grammar, spelling and punctuation _____

Possible points = _____

3. Written & Oral Report (Verbal)

- Follows Oral Report criteria card _____
- Three or more sources used & written in bibliography _____
- Disaster chosen has occurred in past five years _____
- Clear, detailed writing with accurate information _____
- Correct grammar, spelling and punctuation _____

Possible points = _____

4. Newspaper Article (Verbal)

- Writing describes effects on one town or family _____
- Major disaster is clearly described in detail _____
- Includes who, what, when, where, why and how _____
- Historically accurate _____

Suggested extension: Create an entire newspaper that could have been written on the date of this disaster. _____

Possible points = _____

5. Model with Labels (Kinesthetic)

- Follows Model criteria card _____
- Shows entire area of destruction _____
- Volcano's name, country and other facts labeled _____
- Volcano is active _____

Suggested extension: Analyze the effect living around the volcano has on the population. _____

Possible points = _____

6. Information Cube (Kinesthetic)

- Follows Information Cube criteria card _____
- One type of natural disaster is focus of cube _____
- Sides show: Locations, Definition, Effects on People, Destruction Caused, Historic Disasters, Other Facts _____

Suggested extension: Make two or more Information Cubes, each on a different natural disaster. _____

Possible points = _____

7. Slide Show or Photo Montage (Technological)

- Chosen photos clearly show natural disasters _____
- Accurate information about each natural disaster _____
- Four or more types of disasters included _____
- Bibliography of Internet sources used _____

Suggested extension: Show to class and answer questions from your classmates about your information. _____

Possible points = _____

8. WebQuest (Technological)

- Topic of WebQuest is about natural disasters _____
- Work done during the WebQuest is printed out _____
- WebQuest evaluation or rubric is included _____
- Completes evaluation of WebQuest experience _____

Possible points = _____

Assessment of Student Choices _____

_____ Unit

1. _____
Possible points = _____
• • • •

2. _____
Possible points = _____
• • • •

3. _____
Possible points = _____
• • • •

4. _____
Possible points = _____
• • • •

5. _____
Possible points = _____
• • • •

6. _____
Possible points = _____
• • • •

7. _____
Possible points = _____
• • • •

8. _____
Possible points = _____
• • • •

© Pieces of Learning

Tic-Tac-Toe Assessment for <u>Fairy Tales</u>

1. Drawing/painting & List	2. Time Line	3. Skit
Picture clearly shows character ____	Follows Time Line criteria card ____	Follows Skit criteria card ____
Has five character traits on index card ____	Shows five or more main events in fairy tale ____	Setting is present day ____
Character traits are shown in drawing or painting ____	Includes sentence about each event ____	Shows theme clearly ____ Written script is neat with correct spelling/grammar ____
Suggested extension: Compare traits of two different characters in the fairy tale. ____	*Suggested extension: Illustrate your time line showing each event.* ____	*Suggested extension: Perform for another class or entire school.* ____
Possible points = _____	Possible points = _____	Possible points = ____
4. Poem	**5. Letter**	**6. Collage**
Follows Poem criteria card ____	Correct letter format ____ Clearly explains lesson ____	Follows Collage criteria card ____
Format is either a narrative or a lyric poem ____	Shows application to own life ____	Shows setting for 3 fairy tales ____
Retells fairy tale accurately ____	Correct spelling, punctuation and grammar ____	Has words and pictures ____ Creative and original ____
Suggested extension: Put your poem to music and sing for the class. ____	*Suggested extension: Write a new ending to the fairy tale showing a different lesson* ____	*Suggested extension: Include quotes about the setting from the 3+ fairy tales in collage* ____
Possible points = ____	Possible points = ____	Possible points = ____
7. List & Characters	**8. Comic Strip**	**9. Venn Diagram**
Lists 20 character traits ____	Follows Comic Strip criteria card ____	Follows Venn Diagram criteria card ____
Has 3 fairy tale characters for each trait ____	Has characters from 3 or more fairy tales ____	Fairy tale character noted ____
Suggested extension: Write two or three sentences for each trait explaining how the trait affected each character. ____	Plot realistic for characters chosen ____	Traits for yourself and the character are clear ____
	Suggested extension: Write a new fairy tale in a comic book using these characters. ____	*Suggested extension: Write a two page paper comparing and contrasting yourself and the character you have chosen.* ____
Possible points = ____	Possible points = ____	Possible points = ____

Points for Activities: #____=____ pts., #____=____pts., #____=____pts.

Name _____ **Total points** _____ **Grade** _____

Comments:

Tic-Tac-Toe

Tic-Tac-Toe Assessment for _____

1.	2.	3.
4.	5.	6.
7.	8.	9.

Points for Activities: #____=____ pts., #____=____pts., #____=____pts.

Name _____ Total points _____ Grade _____

Comments:

Helpful Hints: Assessment in a Differentiated Classroom

1. Find out what students already know before you begin teaching.

2. Allow students to work on alternate activities when they have mastered the concepts that are being taught.

3. Give guidelines and criteria for success before students begin working and as they work on a task or assignment.

4. Assess often in order to guide students toward academic progress and mastery, not just for points and grades.

5. Follow the guidelines listed below whenever you write a complex rubric, mini-rubric or assessment checklist.

Guidelines for a Good Rubric

➢ Focuses on the standards and learning outcomes

➢ Is understandable to the student

➢ Can be used by the student as a guide for doing quality work

➢ Has no more than 5 levels and no more than 6 criteria

➢ Challenges students to go beyond expectations

➢ Can be used by the teacher to grade coherently and fairly

➢ Can be used to defend the grade if questioned by a student or parent

Norming Rubrics Used to Assess Student Products and Performances

We often hear about norming the scores on standardized tests. On the other hand, it is unusual to hear about rubrics that have been normed. Yet this seems to be an excellent idea for schools where rubrics are used routinely and differentiation is the approach employed in most classrooms.

Norming rubrics is basically about the issue of fairness. Teachers who use a rubric to score the same type of product from a number of different students need to be consistent from one product to the next. When more than one teacher is using the same rubric, the scores should generally be the same from teacher to teacher. A norming session helps teachers understand the rubrics they are using and helps their assessments become more consistent.

In a norming session, teachers:

➢ Review the rubric.
➢ Look at samples of student products.
➢ Individually assign a score to each sample.
➢ Discuss their individual scores with each other.

The purpose of the norming session is to calibrate scores among the group members so that as much consensus as possible results when these group members individually assess student products. Teachers involved in a norming session generally use group discussion about scores to help everyone interpret the rubric and the characteristics of particular product samples.

Preparing for a Norming Session

1. Choose at least seven or eight student products as samples. The samples should all be for the same assignment. The number of sample student products you'll need will vary. You should have at least one representative product for the highest and one for the lowest scores on the rubric used during the norming session. You should also have a couple of products that mark the grade-level range of your rubric.

2. Choose at least one product that stirs up controversy, that is, a student product that will probably receive a wide range of scores from different evaluators. If you can find what's called a "4/1" split (meaning that from two different graders the same product received a score of "4" from one evaluator and a "1" from the other), then you've got a great example of a "controversial" product; a "3/1" split is the next best bet.

3. Make copies of the rubric for all participants in the norming session.

Conducting the Norming Session

1. Tell all graders to read the rubric carefully.

2. Ask them to look at and score three products using the rubric. These three products should be a high, middle and low one. Do not give the participants this information, however.

3. When everyone is finished, decide which of the three products you want to discuss first. Ask each person to announce his or her score to the group. Don't discuss the scores yet, just record them on the board or make a note to yourself and ask the graders to do the same.

4. Ask the most experienced grader to explain his or her reasons for assigning that particular score. Make sure he or she gives specific characteristics of the product and refers to the rubric to support the reasons for assigning a particular score.

5. Ask for discussion among the group members about their various scores. At this point, all group members can and should discuss their individual explanations for their scores. Ask the graders to use specific aspects of the student products and of the rubric to explain their reasons for assigning a particular score.

6. As the facilitator, it best not to offer your opinion about which score is right. If, however, group members' conversation gets overly heated or their debates cannot be resolved, you can mediate their discussion by calling on the people with the most experience and/or whose scores seem most reasonable to you.

7. Don't let individuals over-generalize about the products or criteria; insist that they refer to the rubric and to some specific features of the student products they are discussing. The point of this session is for group members to norm themselves, not for you to get them to conform to what you or one other group member thinks.

8. Repeat this process with the other student products.

9. End with the most controversial product, that is, the one you predict will get the widest range of scores.

10. By the end of this session, participants should understand much more about using rubrics and how to grade students fairly and accurately with them. They should be ready to apply this knowledge when grading their own students' work and should have relatively reliable consistency in the scores they give.

Tiering Summative Assessments

While we often think of tiering student activities and assignments as a differentiation strategy, we seldom think of tiering the final (summative) test for a unit of work. Doing this, however, is beneficial to many students and takes the concept of differentiation to a whole new level.

If the purpose of the test is to assess mastery of a particular skill or standard and to show us how much each student knows, the 'all or nothing' method used in most tests may not be the best approach. In a tiered test, each student has leveled choices to make for each problem or question.

A tiered test or quiz is formatted as a table with rows and columns. The rows are labeled (Row 1, Row 2, Row 3, etc.) as are the columns (Level 1, Level 2 and Level 3). The grade level problems or questions are placed in column #2. Then the teacher creates the same number and type of problems for Level 1 and Level 3. These will go in column #1 and column #3 respectively. Level 1 questions indicate minimal understanding of the standard while Level 3 questions are more challenging and require higher levels of thinking and more advanced knowledge or skills in order to answer them.

All students are required to answer all of the Level 2 questions. These are questions the average student working on grade level should be able to answer with 80% accuracy or higher. Once a student answers all of the Level 2 questions, he/she goes back to Row 1 and begins a process of self-evaluation. If he feels confident that he has answered the Level 2 question correctly, he should attempt to do the Level 3 question. On the other hand, if he feels unsure about his answer to the Level 2 question, he should try Level 1.

The same procedure is followed throughout the entire test. When the test is finished, two questions in each row will be completed. When grading a tiered test or quiz, the teacher counts the highest level question that is answered correctly in each row. In general, the higher the level the more points the item is worth.

While this is usually done on a summative instrument, it also provides formative data for every student, showing some basic knowledge (Level 1) or higher levels of knowledge (Level 3) in addition to the more standardized right or wrong answers of Level 2.

On the next page you will see an example of a tiered math quiz. On the following pages are step-by-step directions and a blank form for writing your own tiered tests and quizzes.

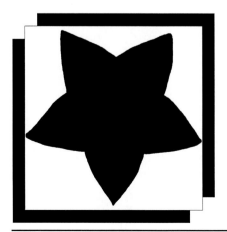

Math Quiz

Multiplication 3-1, 3-2,, 3-6

Name _____ Period _____

General Directions: Browse through the entire quiz. First do each problem in the Level #2 column following the directions. Next, go back to the beginning and evaluate how you think you did on the problem printed in Row #1. If you feel confident in your answer for the Level #2 question, then complete the Level #1 question in that row. Proceed in the same fashion for each row for this section of the quiz. When finished with this section, two questions in each row should be completed. The highest level of question completed accurately will determine your grade in this section of the quiz.

Directions for Level #1, Level #2, and **Level #3.** Solve for **a**. Use mental math and your knowledge of the commutative/associative properties to find the missing number.

	Level #1	Level #2	Level #3
Row #1	200 x 3 = a a =	80 x 80 = a a =	700 x 800 = a a =
Row # 2	40 x 30 = a a =	(2 x 10) x 7 = a a =	50 x (2 x 27) = a a =
Row # 3	900 x 90 = a a =	4 x 9 x 5 = a a =	25 x (16 x 8) = a a =
Row # 4	5,000 x 600 = a a =	4 x (25 x 19) = a a =	60 x 50 x 100 x 10 = a a =
Row # 5	40 x a = 160,000 a =	40 x a = 20,000 a =	25 x 25 x 4 x 12 = a a =

How to Write Tiered Tests and Quizzes

1. Decide what standards, benchmarks and skills will be assessed on the test or quiz.

2. Use the computer to create a table with 3 columns and the number of rows to correspond to the number of questions on the test.

3. Leave space at the top of the paper for the students' name, test directions, etc.

4. Write directions for the test, making it clear that students are to do all Level 2 questions first before starting on either of the other levels.

5. Create a grade level test to assess mastery of the standards and benchmarks you have identified. These items will become Level 2 items on the tiered test.

6. Develop Level 1 (easier) and Level 3 (more challenging) items to correspond with each of the questions on the test.

7. Decide if you want to include any traditional (non-tiered) questions or problems on the test.

8. Assign point values to each leveled question. Point values are decided at your discretion. In general, points for Level 2 should reflect that these are the grade level expectations. Most teachers make Level 3 questions worth more than Level 1, but this needs to be your decision. You should take into account the grading system in your school or district, student motivation, parental understanding of differentiation and the nature of learning differences in your students.

Use the form on the next page to write your own tiered test or quiz.

_____ **Test**

Name _____ **Date** _____

General Directions: Look through the entire test. Then do every question or problem in the Level 2 column. When you have finished, go back to the first problem. Evaluate yourself. If you feel confident you have answered the first problem correctly, do Row 1 in column 3. If you are not sure about your answer, do Row 1 in column 1. Continue with this procedure for the entire test. When you are finished, two questions in each row should be completed.

Level 1	Level 2	Level 3
Row 1		
Row 2		
Row 3		
Row 4		
Row 5		
Row 6		
Row 7		
Row 8		
Row 9		
Row 10		

Grading in the Differentiated Classroom

"For science I hope I get Ms. Crosby," Madison confided to her mom as she got ready for her first day of middle school. "Everyone says she's an 'Easy A'. I definitely don't want to get Mr. Atkinson. He's a really hard grader!"

Grading is one of the strangest and least standardized things we do in education. Every teacher has his or her own method of counting and recording points and deciding what will be important in the final grade. Kids, like Madison in the scenario above, quickly figure out that a grade in one teacher's class does not indicate the same amount of work or effort that the same grade may denote in another teacher's class.

When we differentiate our curriculum and instruction, questions and considerations about grading become even more complex. When all students are not doing the same work, how do we grade them fairly? Throughout this chapter I have shown ways to design rubrics, mini-rubrics and criteria cards. Using these instruments will definitely help you to grade differentiated products and performances. Basing your criteria on grade level standards and benchmarks provides evidence that students have mastered them even if they are doing different work to demonstrate their mastery.

Students should know the Essential Questions for the unit and be able to articulate Enduring Understandings based on what they have learned. Grading within a unit of work should reflect which students know and understand what the unit was about!

Some students may take longer than others to master the standards. Some may need to redo assignments or take tests over again. If grades are based on mastering the standards, it is better to take the higher score that indicates mastery rather than averaging the lower grades together with the higher one.

All students should be making progress and learning new things. Since all students do not start at the same place in either knowledge or skills, we need to indicate how much each has learned. A student who gets 100% on every test but has learned nothing new is not making any progress, yet often gets A's on the report card!

A more challenging concern arises when students are doing work at different tiers or levels. Should students working at a lower level and on less complex tasks be able to earn the same grade as students working at the highest level and on more complex tasks? This is a decision that needs to be made by a grade level or an entire school. There should be an agreement as to how this will be handled that is consistent from teacher to teacher and from grade level to grade level. Both parents and students need to understand how the grading works when students are working on leveled tasks.

To come to consensus on this matter, teachers need to meet together, discuss their thoughts, work their way through potential problems and arrive at a grading system or policy everyone can work with. On the next page you will find a form that you can use to help guide your discussions on this important issue.

Teacher Reflection Questions
Thinking About Grading in a Differentiated Classroom

Grades should reflect mastery of benchmarks and standards and/or indicate progress toward specific learning goals. Think about your method of grading and how you might want to adapt or change it. Discuss these issues with other teachers.

1. How do your grades show mastery of benchmarks or standards?

2. What are your thoughts about what should be counted in the final report card grade?

3. Are things such as effort, behavior, attitude and work habits included in your grades? If so, how do you include them? If not, explain why you do not include them.

4. When students are working on the same learning objectives, benchmarks or standards but are doing different levels of assignments (more difficult and less difficult tasks), how is this handled in your grades?

5. How is individual student progress and/or the results of peer or self assessment included in your grades?

6. Do parents understand how grading is done in your school or classroom? What are some strategies for increasing their understanding in this area?

To Summarize . . .
Differentiated Assessment

➤ Assessment has an important function in differentiation. We use it to learn what our students have mastered and what they still need to know. We use it for flexible grouping and to see growth and progress over time.

➤ Three types of assessments that play an important role in differentiating instruction are pre-assessments, formative assessments and summative assessments.

➤ Knowing how to develop assessment criteria is extremely important in assessing differentiated student products and performances. Listing standards, learning outcomes and assessment criteria is the beginning point for developing a rubric.

➤ Good rubrics give students guidelines for doing quality work and can be used by the teacher to assess and grade student work fairly and coherently.

➤ Complex rubrics have a scale of possible points, a list of targeted criteria and descriptors for each level.

➤ Product and Process Criteria Cards can be used multiple times with different subject areas and content. They are a user-friendly assessment short cut.

➤ Mini-rubrics can be used to assess student products when students have choice of activities such as in an ILP™ or Tic-Tac-Toe.

➤ A session to norm rubrics gives teachers guidelines for using rubrics and provides consistency in grading between teachers.

➤ Summative assessments can be tiered on three levels.

➤ Grading in a differentiated classroom is challenging and must be thought through by all teachers in a grade level, department or school

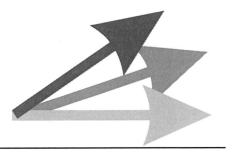

Other Strategies for Differentiation

Technology

Mini-Classes

Mentors

Literature Circles

Questivities™

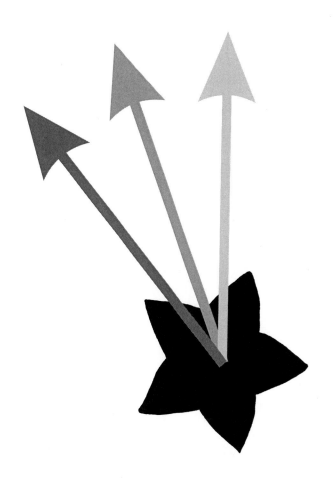

Technology as a Differentiation Tool

Technology seems to be a perfect tool for differentiation. In their lives outside of school, students individualize everything from the music they hear to the pictures they see to the games they play. Their friends may be everyone they've met on MySpace and the videos they see may originate on YouTube. They read blogs they consider interesting even though they may never read a book. They log onto websites, play intricate computer games, create videos and music, and communicate with each other in a myriad of ways. The list is endless.

All of this new technology may intimidate some teachers, but many of our students find using it as natural as breathing! Indeed, their experiences outside of school are already differentiated through technology. They continuously use it in all aspects of their lives. When they do, they are fully engaged in learning.

In the same way, using technology in school has the potential to provide teachers with a number of wonderful tools for differentiating curriculum and instruction. It can benefit students by streamlining their learning, motivating them, and providing a more personalized and flexible approach to education. On the other hand, technology comes with some challenges. It may be difficult for teachers to adjust to various new technologies and to keep up with constant technological innovations. Additionally, some schools have very little technological hardware or software, thus it is hard for these schools to make much use of it.

Recognizing both its benefits and its drawbacks, we need to combine technology with the other teaching strategies we use in a differentiated classroom.

One technological tool that works well in differentiating instruction is **computer assisted instruction.** It automatically adjusts the pace and level of learning for each student and is infinitely patient when a student struggles to learn something. It can be used for remediation of skills or for acceleration and extension of knowledge.

There are many commercially developed programs as well as online resources that use technology in this way. The outcome is personalized, differentiated instruction because the computer continually changes the instruction to fit each student.

Computerized adaptive testing works in much the same way. Test questions become easier or more difficult depending on the answers the student gives. This results in much less frustration for the student and allows the teacher to use test data to pinpoint student needs. Computer adaptive testing takes the concept of tiered assessment discussed in the last chapter and individualizes it even more. It has the potential to track the learning progress of every child.

In general, many of the new information technologies can have a huge effect on teaching and learning. From online courses and videoconferencing to interactive whiteboards and wireless laptops, they can have a major impact as schools look for ways to differentiate curriculum, instruction and assessment.

Technologically savvy students, dubbed 'digital natives' by Marc Prensky, can be our best resource in showing us how to use technology to differentiate in the classroom. Listen to them and ask them questions to learn about the latest gadgets and systems. Brainstorm with them to get ideas about how to best use all available technology to make learning accessible, relevant and stimulating.

Model being a learner as you learn from them. Your willingness to do this will show them that learning new things is not threatening after all! Instead, confirm for them that it is exciting and motivating.

Find out what technologies they are using outside of school and ask questions such as:

➢ What websites have you seen that can give us more information on this topic?
➢ Is what we are doing now similar to something you have done on your computer at home?
➢ Is there a video game that works like this?
➢ Who would like to write a blog on this topic and post it on our classroom website?
➢ Who can take some digital photos to show examples of this idea?
➢ Can anyone find a WebQuest to help us learn more about this topic?

There are many links and many ways you can differentiate through these kinds of questions. The information that students are exposed to on a daily basis is enormous and much more differentiated from student to student than it was in the 20th century. Have them share what they know and what they have discovered via technology. All students benefit from this array of knowledge.

Using Technology for Data Analysis

Data management and analysis can help us pinpoint students who need help learning specific skills. It allows us to comb through assessment results and single out a student or group of students who need to learn a particular standard or benchmark. Using technological tools, we can analyze student performance in ways we couldn't even have dreamed of a few years ago. This can lead to differentiation with more individualized teaching of specific knowledge and skills.

Based on the data, teachers can flexibly group and regroup students according to the skills they have mastered and those they need to learn. With technology, data can be given to teachers quickly so they can work on problems as soon as they arise.

Some systems keep track of each standardized test question, the skill it measures and each student's answer. By matching student errors with the skills tested, the system can show who knows what. Such systems can also spot weaknesses in an entire class. This gives teachers information about what most of his or her students do not understand.

Good achievement-tracking technology can:

• Show which skills individual students have and have not mastered
• Spot problems with certain skills that most students in a class are having
• Show strengths and weaknesses of individual teachers
• Give parents information to see how their child is doing

Using technology for data analysis is a practical strategy that can give us helpful information. It is not, however, a 'magic bullet' and can only give us information as valuable as the data it analyzes. There are still many things data analysis cannot do. It cannot grade or assess authentic assessments such as projects or essays. It cannot determine why certain students are doing well while others are doing poorly. It cannot give teachers strategies they need to use to differentiate for groups or individuals. Thus, it is just one of many tools we need to use as we differentiate instruction, curriculum and assessment.

Online Courses and Virtual Schools

Another use of technology as a tool for differentiation is the creation of online courses and virtual schools. Such schools allow students to work at their own pace from home or at a location most convenient for them. Online courses offer students both variety in course selection and flexibility in time requirements. Both work well in meeting specific student needs. While colleges and universities have offered online courses for a number of years, virtual schooling and online coursework is now an option for K-12 students.

Virtual schools are excellent avenues for differentiation because they can offer curriculum based on individual needs. Younger students can do more advanced coursework if appropriate. Students who need remediation can have individualized instruction based on their needs. Timing can be customized to meet students' schedules or pace of learning. Some virtual schools deliver the entire curriculum via the Internet while others combine face-to-face contact with online studies. In either case, the curriculum is differentiated for each student.

Virtual schools and online learning are chosen for a variety of different reasons:

- A student is functioning significantly above or below his grade level peers
- A student has a disability and needs an individualized program
- A student has a chronic health problem and cannot attend school
- A student is bullied in a regular school setting
- A student wants to take courses not offered by the local school
- A student in an urban area finds the local school too dangerous
- A student is an athlete, actor or musician whose schedule doesn't allow him to attend school during regular hours

As is true in a face-to-face context, planning instruction for a virtual school, an online course or an individual student takes a great deal of thought and time. Written instructions, lectures and online discussion groups plus the use of videos, websites and other online resources must be carefully designed and coordinated. The hardware and software at each site must be checked by someone with technological expertise. Expectations for learning must be clearly delineated for each student.

With these details in place, online learning is an excellent way to differentiate and meet individual student needs.

WebQuests

Using WebQuests is another excellent way to differentiate curriculum via technology. They were developed in early 1995 by Bernie Dodge at San Diego State University. According to Dodge, a WebQuest "is an inquiry-oriented activity in which most or all of the information used by learners is drawn from the Web. WebQuests are designed to use learners' time well, to focus on using information rather than looking for it, and to support learners' thinking at the levels of analysis, synthesis and evaluation."

Since WebQuests were first introduced, thousands of them have been developed by teachers and posted on various websites as resources for others. Because there are so many excellent examples of WebQuests, teachers using them are able to learn from each other. WebQuests infuse technology into the curriculum and are excellent learning tools.

A good WebQuest has:

➢ Guidance and clear directions for students
➢ A creative and flexible final product or project
➢ Working website links for research and information
➢ Relevant and up-to-date information
➢ A design that lets students work independently

WebQuests develop research skills by giving students a task that allow them to draw on their imagination and problem solving skills. Using WebQuests, students do not merely copy and print out information. Because the answers are not predefined, students use creative and critical thinking to figure out solutions to the problems that are posed. Students explore a topic in depth in a structured and meaningful way and find their own answers, especially when the topic is multi-faceted and has no obvious right and wrong answer.

WebQuests can be developed to accommodate students' diverse learning needs. Special needs students can work on a WebQuest with a group when they are given predetermined tasks based on their abilities and readiness. Gifted and other high ability students can extend the basic WebQuest tasks in much the same way extensions were shown in the previous chapter.

To develop your own WebQuest, start by looking at some that have been developed by others. Make note of what you like and what you don't like in the ones you see. Use Dodge's six building blocks of a WebQuest as a structure for writing your own:

1. **The Introduction** – Orients students and captures their interest.

2. **The Task** – Describes the goal and end product of the activity.

3. **The Process** – Explains the strategies students should use to complete the task.

4. **The Resources** – Links to the websites used to complete the task.

5. **The Evaluation** – Assesses and measures the results of the activity.

6. **The Conclusion** – Sums up the activity and encourages student reflection.

Top 10 Reasons We Should Use Technology to Differentiate Instruction

1. There are wide gaps in student experience and ability. Technology can help us locate the gaps and bridge them.

2. Students are motivated when they use technology.

3. Technology is a huge part of students' learning outside of the classroom. We need to use it in the classroom as well.

4. Technological applications tend to be very flexible and can be targeted to each student's individual needs.

5. Technology is everywhere in the "real world". Using technology in the classroom helps to prepare our students for the world beyond the classroom.

6. The knowledge that each student has differs greatly. Having students share what they know and what they have learned via technology benefits everyone.

7. Technology is very efficient and is often a time-saver for teachers stretched by having too much to do and too little time to do it.

8. We handle a large amount of data and information about individual students, test results and curriculum requirements. Technology can help us sort and select this and make it more manageable and useful.

9. Knowledge changes rapidly, almost from day to day and hour to hour. Technology allows us to keep up with the changes as they occur and gives us the most up-to-date information.

10. We can show students that we are learners as well as teachers, allowing them to teach us things about technology that we don't know.

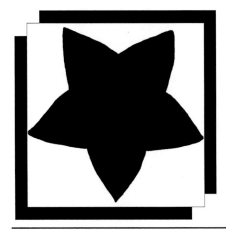

Mentors

Resources to help us differentiate our instruction are everywhere. Sometimes the best human resources – mentors — can be found right in your own town or community. Retired people, those with part time jobs, grandparents or stay-at-home moms and dads are all possibilities for mentors in your school. Sometimes high school students serve as mentors for elementary school children.

The concept of mentoring comes from the ancient Greeks. In ancient times, most educated people had mentors who planned and personalized their learning. Socrates is probably the best known mentor of the ancient world. Due to the development of apprenticeships, mentoring was formalized and institutionalized throughout the Middle Ages.

During this time, a mentor was considered a wiser and more experienced person who passed down his knowledge and skills to the next generation.

Mentors are not just for people of long ago. They are a terrific resource for differentiation in the 21st century. Mentors work on an ongoing basis with an individual student in an area of interest or need. Seek out adults or older students who are willing to work with a student in this way. Good mentors generally need some training, but the most important characteristic is having a love of children and an ability to share knowledge and skills.

This one-on-one relationship benefits both advanced and struggling students. Mentors set an example, offer intellectual stimulation and knowledge, communicate excitement about the learning process and understand individual students and their needs. Mentors share their interests, time, talent and skills. Dependability, patience, flexibility and commitment are the traits to look for in a potential mentor for a student.

Essential to a having excellent mentorship is making sure there is a good match between the mentor and the student. When this happens, the mentorship becomes a shared relationship where values, attitudes, passions and traditions are passed from one person to another. It should provide both the mentor and the student with encouragement, inspiration and new insights. A mentor becomes a role model as well as a source for support and encouragement.

Students from disadvantaged populations benefit greatly from mentors. Mentors give these students a feel for the lifestyle associated with their professions and the educational credentials needed for it. Mentors often have a maturing effect on adolescents and support them in reaching their academic and personal goals.

Successful mentorships must be structured and organized in order to function in an optimal way. Mentors need to learn how to interact with children and teenagers. They should be trained in role-modeling skills, goal setting, handling mistakes, and listening skills. They need to learn how to acknowledge and encourage student accomplishments. Usually some type of initial training is offered and ongoing training should also be available. Mentors should commit to work with a student for a certain amount of time. Many schools find that a semester or a year is a good length of time for an initial commitment. Some mentors end up working with their students for years.

Steps to Establishing Good Mentorships

1. Identify student needs.

2. Find out which students want a long-term relationship with a mentor.

3. Identify possible mentors.

4. Interview mentor candidates. Find out how much time they have and whether they are interested in taking on such a commitment.

5. Match students and mentors according to interests and learning styles.

6. Give the students guidelines for working with a mentor. Talk about responsibilities, benefits and expectations for both the student and the mentor.

7. Conduct an initial training session for the mentors.

8. Monitor the mentor relationship for each student with a mentor.

9. Provide ongoing training for the mentors at least four times a year.

10. Assess and evaluate each mentorship after a certain amount of time.

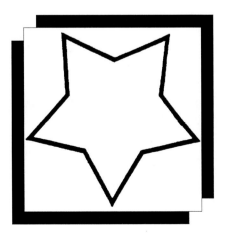

Mini-Classes

Mini-classes are short classes on a wide variety of topics or interest areas. The topics are not generally part of the regular curriculum, but are a wonderful way to broaden our students' vision, increase their interest in new things and expose them to all kinds of new skills, knowledge and information. Mini-classes can be taught by teachers, parents, community volunteers, paraprofessionals, and/or other instructional personnel.

Mini-classes provide a way for you to use community resources to help differentiate your curriculum. Many adults in the community may not be able to mentor a student on a long-term basis but would be more than willing to come to the school once or twice and teach a specialized skill.

These classes are an excellent way to provide enrichment for all students. Students can select classes based on their areas of interest. These classes are a relatively easy way to begin differentiation within your whole school.

Implementing the Mini-Class strategy takes planning. In order to do this planning you need to first consider the questions below. You may also want to use the Mini-Classes Planning Form on the next page.

1. Who needs to approve of offering mini-classes before you can begin planning?

2. Who will be the leader, organizer or facilitator for the mini-class program at your school?

3. What will be the length of time for each mini-class?

4. Will more than one mini-class be offered at the same time?

5. Will this be a one-time offering or an ongoing program?

6. How will mini-classes be advertised?

7. How will students be selected to attend a mini-class?

8. Will mini-classes take place during the school day or will they be offered before school and after school?

9. How will teachers for the mini-classes be recruited?

10. What are some potential topics for mini-classes?

11. How will mini-classes be evaluated?

Mini-Classes Planning Form

Class/Topic	Teacher	Time	Location

Student Selection:

Publicity:

Program Evaluation:

Literature Circles

Literature circles are an excellent strategy for differentiation because they can be designed to meet individual needs by using learning styles, learning modalities and multiple intelligences. They can also be based on reading level, with students reading different books on the same theme or topic but at different levels.

Students who have read a good book want to tell others about it. Literature circles give students a way to share what they have read without resorting to "Round Robin" and whole class discussions.

Literature circles are highly motivating. Students seem to thrive with the independence and responsibility they require. They learn collaboration skills and learn from each other as they discuss and comprehend what they have read. Information from others in the literature circle can reinforce student learning or stretch students in new directions.

There is no 'right' way to structure literature circles. They are as individual as each teacher and his students. In general, students come to the literature circle having already read the story, chapter or book they will be discussing. All students are actively involved in literature circle discussions and each has a specific role.

Roles vary depending upon the number of students in a group, the skill levels of the students and the type of book read. Roles are usually given names that are related to the duties of the role. It is best to have one role for each person in the group. There are many possibilities for roles. Some are suggested below.

Literature Circle Roles

➤ **Discussion Leader** – Runs the daily meeting of the literature circle and keeps the group on task. Makes sure all group activities are completed.

➤ **Secretary** – Records notes from the group discussion and writes the answers to most written activities done by the group.

➤ **Illustrator** – Draws something important from the group's discussion or the assignment.

➤ **Dictionary Expert** – Records vocabulary words and definitions. Focuses on new, difficult or interesting words. Writes any vocabulary activities completed by the group.

➤ **Reflection Expert** – Records the group's predictions for the next day's readings. Evaluates how well the group worked together on a daily basis. Makes suggestions to the group regarding any changes that need to be made.

➤ **Understudy** – Is aware of all of the roles for the group and the responsibilities of each role. Can step in to any role if a group member is absent or unprepared.

In designing the format for any literature circle, planning and preparation are crucial to its' overall success. Many times students choose what they are going to read. Sometimes choices are limited due to reading levels or the appropriateness of the selection for a particular student. All choices need to be appealing and challenging for individual readers.

In their excellent and practical book *Building Literature Circles,* Jimmie Aydelott and Dianna S. Buck recommend both long-range and short-range planning in implementing literature circles. Both types of planning are important before you begin using them in your classroom. On the next three pages, you will find a summary of their planning suggestions.

LONG-RANGE PLANNING

GET READY

1. How will I structure my Literature Circles?

2. When will I schedule Literature Circles?
   - in lieu of a basal text
   - secondary to the basal text
   - alternate with basal text
   - enrichment purposes

3. On what will my Literature Circles focus?
   - genres
   - themes
   - author studies
   - free choice

4. How will I teach the necessary reading skills with Literature Circles?
   - use the skills lessons that are in basal text teachers' guides
   - write my own skills lessons
   - use resource books
   - use Internet sources

5. When will I teach the skills lessons?
   - as separate mini-skills lessons
   - in a focus lesson before each Literature Circle and/or reading session

6. How will I manage the classroom?

7. How will I assess?

8. What books will I use?
   - make a tentative year-long plan

9. Where can I get necessary books that I don't have?
   - public, school and classroom libraries
   - borrow from other teachers
   - purchase

from *Building Literature Circles* © Pieces of Learning

SHORT-RANGE PLANNING

GET SET

This is where you get down to the practical details of getting things together for the Circles. Here are a few things to consider in this phase of your planning and preparation.

Orientation and Training

Orientation and **Training** are prerequisites for successful student-led Literature Circles.

During Orientation, students learn to do the independent activities required in a regular Literature Circle through teaching, modeling and practicing while reading short stories or chapter books. During Training, they learn the different discussion roles through teaching, modeling and practicing while reading short stories or chapter books.

1. Secure short stories or books
2. Read the stories ahead of time
3. Determine time needed
4. Prepare and duplicate role sheets and other material.

Actual Literature Circles . .

1. Determine the time frame for reading, discussion and culminating activities.
2. Secure the books needed for each group.
3. Decide how your group will be formed
   - Teacher Assignment
   - Book choice
4. Read the books.
5. Determine grading criteria and assessment tools you will use.
6. Decide whether to use a group culminating activity.
7. Decide whether you will use additional end-of-book independent activities and, if so, which ones you will use.
8. Duplicate all necessary materials.

from *Building Literature Circles* © Pieces of Learning

GO

Planning is over and you are ready to get started! Here are some helpful hints:

- During the Orientation phase, use short stories or a novel to teach students how to complete the various independent activities that will be required during a Literature Circle (e.g., reader response items, graphic organizers, coded post-its).
- During the Training phase, students learn the different discussion roles, one at a time, while reading short stories or a novel.

1. Establish groups.
2. Hand out and explain materials.
3. On Day 1:
   - meet as a whole class for a focus lesson to review what is expected in the Circle and how to complete the independent activities you may require.
   - groups meet and
     - roles are assigned.
     - role sheets are given out.
     - reading assignments are noted.
4. On Day 2 and until the next predetermined group meeting, students:
   - complete the required reading assignment.
   - complete required independent activities.
5. Next designated circle meeting:
   - students discuss what they read according to their role sheets and notes they have.
   - students ascertain assignment to be read before the next Circle meeting.
   - students exchange roles and get new role sheets.
6. This pattern of reading and meeting is continued until the book has been completed.
7. After the book has been completed, the independent extension activities may be assigned.
8. Last—but not least—groups may plan and present a culminating activity to the whole class. This serves as a closure, as well as an advertisement to future readers.

First Student-Led Literature Circle

from *Building Literature Circles*   © Pieces of Learning

Questivities™

The Questivities™ ('Questioning Activities') format consists of an interdisciplinary Project Activity along with a series of Thinking Questions that stimulate creative and critical thinking and give practice in research skills. The questions are starter questions that should be done before students begin the project itself.

Students who use Questivities™ before doing the Project Activity create projects that reflect higher levels of thinking, more creativity, and more evidence of research. Questivities™ take students beyond just working on a project to thinking about the project ideas in more depth and greater detail.

Questivities™ can be used in many ways. They can be done individually, in partners or in a group setting. They can be a requirement used in conjunction with a project in a differentiated unit of study. They can be used to enhance and extend individual work and research. They can be one of several extension activities in a learning center. Questivities™ also make excellent alternate activities for students who compact out of the regular curriculum.

Questivities™ incorporate Learning Modalities, Learning Styles, Bloom's Taxonomy and Multiple Intelligences. They are assessed using mini-rubrics or other performance assessment criteria. Teachers can write Questivities™ for a unit of study or teach their students how to write and develop them for their own research projects.

Questivities™ are written on a user-friendly one page form. The form has the following elements:

➢ Project Activity which provides the focus for the Questivities™
➢ Learning Modality
➢ Learning Style
➢ Bloom's Taxonomy level
➢ Multiple Intelligences
➢ Assessment Mini-Rubric for the Project Activity
➢ Questivities™ Thinking Questions
➢ Active Question

On the next page you will see a Questivities™ written for a Project Activity on Insects. On the following page is a blank Questivities™ form for you to use to write your own.

Learning Modality

- Kinesthetic

Learning Style

- Concrete Random

Taxonomy Level

- Analysis, Synthesis

Multiple Intelligences

- Verbal/Linguistic
- Bodily/Kinesthetic
- Naturalist

Insects
Questivities™
Project Activity

Create your own insect.
Make a model that includes all of the major characteristics of any insect.
Write a short report explaining what your insect is like.

Assessment Mini-Rubric

- Follows Model criteria card
- New insect has major characteristics of all insects
- Report explains habitat, life processes, food, and effects on environment
- Creativity

Project Questions

- What characteristics do all insects have in common?
- What effects do insects have on the environment?

Questivities™ Thinking Questions

1. List all of the insects you can think of (at least ten).
2. Compare/contrast an ant and a butterfly.
3. What would happen if all of the insects in the world were exterminated?
4. Would you rather be a grasshopper or a hornet? Why?
5. How would you feel if roaches were the only insects left in the world?
6. Why are insects both beneficial and harmful to humans?
7. How will you design a new insect? What kind of insect do you want it to be?

Active Question:
- Make a list of questions a cricket might ask an ant.

Directions: Answer the **Questivities™ Thinking Questions** and the **Active Question** before doing the Project Activity.

Learning Modality

Learning Style

Taxonomy Level

Multiple Intelligence

Assessment Mini-Rubric

Project Questions

> **Questivities™**
> **Project Activity**

Questivities™ Thinking Questions

1. List

2. Compare/contrast

3. What would happen if

4. Would you rather

5. How would you feel if

6. Why

7. How

Active Question:

- Make a list of questions_____might ask _____.

Directions: Answer the **Questivities™ Thinking Questions** and the **Active Question** before doing the Project Activity.

To Summarize . . .
Other Strategies for Differentiation

➢ **Technology** is a wonderful tool to use for differentiation. It can streamline and individualize student learning and provide a more personalized and flexible approach to developing curriculum.

➢ **Computer assisted instruction**, computer adaptive testing, products using technology, data analysis, online courses, virtual schools and classrooms, WebQuests, and independent research are just some of the ways we can use technology in the differentiated classroom.

➢ Using technology wisely requires training and skill. It also means that students need to be engaged in appropriate learning with technology using appropriate resources.

➢ **Mentors** can provide one-on-one relationships for students and offer intellectual stimulation, knowledge, excitement about learning, and an understanding of an individual student and his or her needs. Successful mentorships must be structured and organized in order to function in an optimal way.

➢ **Mini-classes** are short classes on a wide variety of topics or interest areas. They can broaden students' vision and introduce them to a world of new things. Planning how this strategy could be implemented is the first step in using it in your school.

➢ **Literature circles** allow students to discuss the stories and books they are reading in a small group setting. Specific roles are assigned to each person in the group. Both long-term and short-term planning are important to use this strategy effectively.

➢ **The Questivities™** ('Questioning Activities') format is useful in giving students higher level thinking questions to answer before they begin a project activity. Students who use Questivities™ show more depth in their thinking, more creativity and more evidence of research.

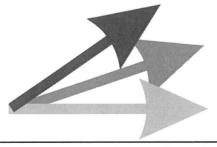

Differentiating for Special Groups and Students

Gifted students
Students with disabilities
English language learners

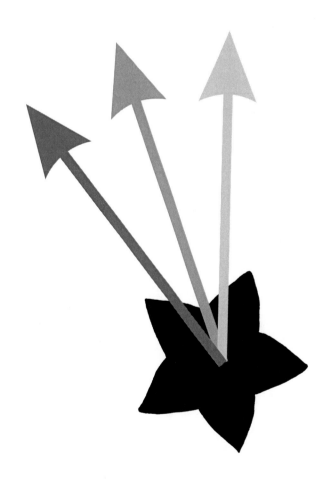

Differentiating for Special Groups and Students

Differentiation is an approach to teaching and learning that works well for all students. It is particularly important, however, when we work with students who vary greatly from the norm or whose needs are far different from others at the same age and grade level. In this chapter we will consider the needs of gifted and talented students, special education students, and English language learners. While the strategies that have been discussed in previous chapters work well with children in these groups, we need to pinpoint their needs and see exactly how these strategies can meet those needs in a differentiated classroom.

Differentiation for Gifted and Talented Students

The concept of differentiation originated with researchers who were looking for ways to meet the needs of gifted students in a regular classroom setting. Many of the strategies discussed throughout this book can be used to meet the needs of the gifted.

Assessment is often the key to providing appropriate learning tasks for gifted students. These assessments can take many forms and often drive differentiated instruction for them. They can be done before a learning task begins or during the learning process itself. They can be used to give students and their parents feedback after a project or performance is completed. Assessments often point the way to the next learning challenge.

For gifted students, doing pre-assessment is essential to see what they already know, but also to find out what they do not know after all. Sometimes we make assumptions that gifted students know more of the curriculum than they actually do. Curriculum Compacting, a strategy discussed in Chapter 3, can be used to delineate the skills that have been mastered. This sets the stage for more advanced work.

It is essential that we show gifted students how to extend their thinking by indicating this within the learning tasks we give them and also within our rubrics or other assessment tools. It is human nature to stop once you think the task has been adequately completed. In a classroom just focused on learning the grade level standards, gifted students often get the idea that learning is easy and school is boring.

Instead, our gifted students should be given the message that learning is ongoing and life long, with benchmarks along with way that lead to new challenges and opportunities. Because gifted students frequently know much of the regular curriculum, one approach to teaching them is to give them more advanced work and more complex problems to solve.

By working with such problems, they can learn new skills in self-directed learning, thinking, research and communication. The way gifted students demonstrate these skills is generally through innovative products and performances that are individual in nature, creative and of high quality.

One problem that may come up when you give gifted students more challenging work is that they and their parents seem to be more concerned about points and grades than they are about the learning itself. It is important for them to understand that in the long run, lifelong learning is the goal.

You will probably need to educate both the students and their parents about the benefits of differentiation and why it is important for them to do more demanding work. Make sure your grading system is set up in such a way that the students doing the hardest work are not receiving the lowest grades in the class. If you do not, grading will create problems with students and parents alike!

Differentiation for gifted students should begin by looking at the needs of individual students. Not all gifted students are alike, and their needs differ greatly. On the next page you will find a chart that lists common needs and concerns about gifted students and corresponding strategies and techniques that can be used to differentiate the curriculum and meet these needs.

The strategies listed are ones we have already discussed in this book. Think through them again as you consider the needs of your gifted and talented students.

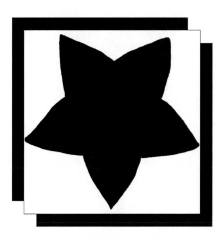

DIFFERENTIATION FOR GIFTED STUDENTS

Needs and Concerns		Strategies and Techniques
1. Student already knows the skill or concept that is being taught.	→	❑ Flexible Grouping ❑ Curriculum Compacting ❑ Learning Contract ❑ Collaboration with other teachers
2. Student will learn the information, skills and/or concepts faster than most others in the class.	→	❑ Independent study ❑ Become a resident expert on some facet of the topic ❑ Thematic Units
3. Student could become interested in the topic, but the teaching style does not match his learning style.	→	❑ Individual Lesson Plans™(ILP) based on Learning Styles, Learning Modalities and / or Multiple Intelligences
4. Student does not feel she is being academically or intellectually challenged.	→	❑ Questivities™ ❑ ILPs™ at the higher levels of Bloom's Taxonomy ❑ Enrichment activities that involve real life problem solving ❑ Acceleration strategies ❑ Tiered Lesson/Units
5. Student has given up on school, is unmotivated, wants to be entertained rather than work.	→	❑ Pursuit of special interest area ❑ Personal interest and attention from one "special teacher" ❑ Personal goal setting ❑ Development of self-confidence

Differentiation for Students with Disabilities

Special education teachers usually know a great deal about differentiation even if they have had very little training in it. This is because special education programs have always looked to the individual needs of students. Such programs have focused on diagnostic testing, individual short and long term goals and a host of strategies for children who don't learn as well using traditional teaching methods.

With many special education students now being served in regular classroom settings, it is important for all teachers to understand how to differentiate for this group of students. The key to doing this is being able to modify and adapt your instruction, materials, content, assignments and assessments. That is a big order for any teacher!

In order to differentiate for special needs students, you need to review your curriculum regularly and target instruction to meet their individual needs. Make sure you have materials with a variety of levels and tiered assignments so that these students can learn. Ask the special education teacher at your school for materials that you can use with these students. Giving them work that is too difficult only brings about frustration for them and for you.

As with gifted students discussed previously, use pre-assessment to find out what your special needs students already know. Make connections between this and the new content you are introducing. Monitor how well they are integrating their prior knowledge with new information. Remember that it may take more repetitions for these students to learn new concepts and skills than it takes for regular education students. Modify your instruction by building in more time for these students to learn the most important standards and skills.

Use graphic organizers, more visuals, active learning and hands-on activities as much as possible. Be intentional about study skills and memorization techniques that will help them remember new information. Use pairs and partners and peer tutoring as needed.

Many teachers are concerned about special education students learning the grade level standards. As much as is feasible, align the individual student goals stated in each IEP with the grade level standards you are teaching. Then examine various differentiation strategies to determine which ones to use to meet both the IEP goals and the standards you are to teach. Using a Venn diagram will help you to see the connections between the two. Make use of the form on the next page as you think through your approaches to doing this.

Aligning IEP Goals and State Standards

Name of Student _____

IEP Goal(s)

State Standards

Connections between them:

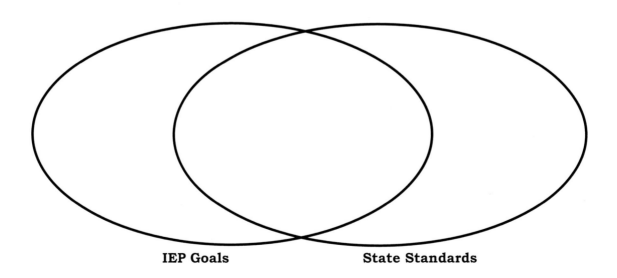

IEP Goals   State Standards

© Pieces of Learning

Reading, Math, NCLB, and Students with Disabilities

Because of the requirements of No Child Left Behind (NCLB) and the fact that literacy is essential for everyone in the 21st century Information Age, many teachers are focused on improving the reading and math skills of students with disabilities. Some strategies for doing this in the differentiated classroom are as follows:

1. Model oral reading skills and give these students a variety of ways to practice.

2. Make sure reading selections are at the students' independent reading level if they are going to read something on their own.

3. Teach vocabulary through oral language and general classroom discussion.

4. Repeat exposure to new words.

5. Demonstrate how to think while reading. When reading a story, stop and ask for thoughts, predictions and connections to other learning.

6. Work on basic skills in phonemic awareness and phonics.

7. Show students how reading skills are connected to other skill and content areas. Make the connections obvious for these students.

8. Use literature circles to promote discussion about and comprehension of what has been read.

9. Emphasize memorization of basic math facts, algorithms and formulas.

10. Connect reading and math skills and demonstrate using both to solve math word problems.

11. Adapt the amount of work required depending on the pace of individual students' learning.

12. Use technological tools such as computer assisted instruction and computer adapted testing to individualize instruction for your disabled students. (See Chapter 8 for more information.)

Many of the strategies you have read about in this book target the needs of special education students. Especially appropriate are:

➢ Flexible grouping

Students with disabilities benefit from many types of groupings. They need homogeneous groups for specific skill development. Literature circles help with reading skills and comprehension. Heterogeneous groups improve social and academic skills.

➢ Learning profiles and preferences

Understanding learning style strengths and weaknesses, which modalities work best with a certain student and which of the multiple intelligences he or she has helps in differentiating products and performances that these students can do.

➢ Tiered lessons and units

Tiered activities that focus on the grade level standards are very helpful for students with disabilities. When the learning activity is doable, the frustration level for these students goes down! Tiered units also include some whole class activities and many times some heterogeneous grouping. This combination works well for these students.

➢ Differentiated assessments

Use the results of daily classroom activities to monitor student progress. Give brief timed tests or quizzes and graph them so that both you and the student can visually see the progress he or she is making. Use criteria cards and rubrics as well as diagnostic tests. Use computer adaptive testing to give you data about individual student progress.

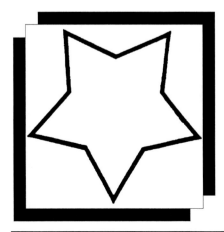

Differentiation for English Language Learners

Students whose first language is not English can be found in nearly every American school. Many of them do not speak English well enough to follow the standard curriculum unless we use differentiation strategies targeted to meet their needs. Even when these students have learned basic social English, they may struggle with the academic English needed in the classroom.

Part of differentiating for English Language Learners is being intentional about teaching them **academic English**. This includes focusing on:

> ➢ Words that describe general content and subject area knowledge
>
> ➢ Words that are specific to the vocabulary of the unit being studied
>
> ➢ Words that explain the required learning processes in the unit

Some specific strategies to use with these students are:

1. Use body movements, gestures, facial expressions along with words to ensure they understand what you are talking about.

2. Use manipulatives and other hands-on learning techniques.

3. Talk more slowly and use shorter sentences.

4. Avoid idioms and slang. Many ELL students do a literal translation of such expressions and therefore don't know what you are talking about!

5. Present work in smaller amounts and give these students more time to complete the assignments.

6. Include lots of visuals such as charts, graphs, maps, diagrams and pictures to convey the information to the students.

7. Use flash cards with a picture on the front and words on the back.

8. Show examples of good projects and good work so that they can see and understand classroom expectations.

9. Use the visual and kinesthetic modalities to teach concepts and ideas.

10. Use the Unit Planner found on the next two pages to plan ways to differentiate a unit of study for your English Language Learners.

Unit Planner to Differentiate for English Language Learners

Title of Unit_____

Grade/Subject_____Time frame for Unit_____

List main topics in this unit.

What standards will be covered in this unit?

What questions should students be able to answer after completing this unit?

What aspects of English do students need to know to complete the classroom tasks for this unit? (Example: Take notes, compare/contrast, present orally)

What are the major terms or academic/technical vocabulary students need to know in this unit?

What are the major assignments in this unit? Can any be modified?

What background knowledge in the topic should students have to be successful in this unit? How can this background be taught if students don't have it?

List resources and materials these students should use in this unit.

How can English Language Learners (and others who struggle with language skills) be encouraged to join class discussion during this unit?

How will learning be assessed for this unit? Can any assessments be modified?

To Summarize . . .
Differentiating for Special Groups and Students

➢ Pre-assessment is essential in differentiating for gifted students. We need to see what they know and also what they do not know. This is the basis for beginning instruction.

➢ Differentiation for gifted students should focus on self-directed learning, thinking skills, research and communication. Skills should be demonstrated through innovative products and performances that are creative and of high quality.

➢ Differentiation strategies can be targeted to meet specific needs that gifted students may have.

➢ The key to differentiating for special education students is modifying and adapting instruction, materials, content, assignments and assessments.

➢ Correlate IEP goals and grade-level standards to see how you can affect both.

➢ English Language Learners need to specifically understand the academic English required in a unit of study in order to be successful learners.

➢ Use visuals, gestures, demonstrations, pictures and hands-on learning along with words in order to increase understanding of what is being taught.

➢ The Unit Planner to Differentiate for English Language Learners is a comprehensive planner for differentiation of a unit of study. This same planner works well in planning for learning disabled students.

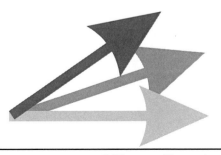

Keys to Successful
Schoolwide
or
Districtwide Differentiation

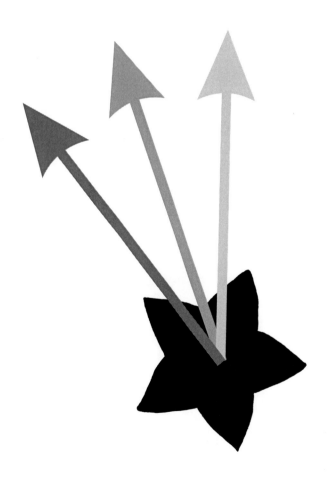

Keys to Successful Schoolwide or Districtwide Differentiation

Knowing how to differentiate curriculum and instruction is an essential skill for any teacher in the 21st century. However, training teachers to differentiate doesn't happen overnight. It is a long process that takes time, effort, planning, practice, ongoing teacher training and a wealth of practical strategies that teachers can implement effectively. These are the elements that turn the concept of differentiation into a reality.

A first step is to help teachers understand that their students most certainly do have special and unique needs. The next step is to show them practical and doable ways to meet these needs. This challenge is one that can be met by using the strategies inherent in differentiation.

While most educators acknowledge that they have not been issued "standardized students" and therefore agree that differentiation is a great idea in principle, the pressing question usually is: "How do you actually implement this concept in a school or school district?" Such an undertaking is a challenge! While one workshop or a pep talk about "Differentiation for All" may spark the initial interest of a few teacher-leaders, this at best is merely the spark to get the fire going.

In this chapter we will look at some structured ways to plan and implement differentiation in your school or school district. We will explore some general guidelines and time lines and look at sample training agendas. This should be helpful in giving you a starting point for thinking and planning. All of these can be personalized and adapted to meet your specific needs.

We will begin by looking at fourteen general guidelines. Following that, you will see two sample training agendas. One is for four sessions done over the course of one school year. The other is a three year plan. Both of these can serve as examples as you write your own.

Later in this chapter you will see lists delineating traits to look for in an Administrator, Outside Consultant and In-House Expert to help in implementing your schoolwide or districtwide plan. You will also find some information about organizing Demonstration Classrooms that showcase various differentiation strategies. Finally, we will take a look at some 'Nuts and Bolts' issues and a reproducible list of ideas for parents suggesting ways for them to support differentiation in their child's classroom.

General Guidelines for Schools or Districts

1. Begin with the most eager and motivated teachers. These are usually the early adapters of new ideas and they will get the ball rolling in your school or district!

2. Start small and build from there. A small group of enthusiastic teachers who are focused on implementing a concept and armed with several practical classroom strategies will set the stage for more encompassing change throughout your school or school district.

3. Have a plan for continually incorporating more teachers into professional development activities.

4. Make use of conference sessions or short introductory workshops as beginning motivators, starting points or interest builders for teachers. However, don't expect that a great deal of on going change will come as a result of these alone.

5. Remember that effective professional development for teachers is high quality, sustained, intensive and classroom-focused. (Section 9101.34 of NCLB)

6. Have a comprehensive plan that includes several training sessions plus time for writing new units and strategies, sharing with one another and follow-up after new strategies have been tried in the classroom. (See sample agenda on page 208 and the Plan for Schoolwide Differentiation form on page 215.)

7. Whenever possible, supply teachers with books or other resources that they can use in the workshop and then reference later to make the implementation of what they have learned easier.

8. Make certain principals and other administrators support differentiation and are actively involved in the professional development of teachers. Even if they cannot attend the training, their interest and backing is crucial. (See Traits of a Good Administrator on page 212.)

9. Use an outside consultant who understands the practical needs and concerns of teachers. While theory may be relevant and worthwhile, teachers need to come away from the training with practical strategies showing them how to actually implement and use the concept in their classrooms. (See Traits of a Good Outside Consultant on page 213.)

10. Develop in-house resident experts who are willing to organize and facilitate regularly scheduled follow-up sessions. (See Traits of Good In-House Resident Experts on page 214.)

11. Showcase classrooms where differentiation strategies are being used well. Build in time for workshop participants to see these classrooms in action. Consider developing a Demonstration Classroom Program in your school or district. (See Developing a Demonstration Classroom Program and the Demonstration Teacher Information Form on pages 217.)

12. Acknowledge and talk about the change process within the school and school culture.

13. Involve and educate parents so that they have a good understanding of differentiation, including what it is, how it works and the effect it has on their child's learning.

14. Become self-sustaining and able to incorporate and train new teachers as they come into the school or school district.

Differentiation Training – Sample Four-Day Agenda

Day 1

- Introduction to Differentiation
- Flexible grouping
- Curriculum compacting
- Learning contracts
- Anchoring activities
- Structuring independent study
- Tiered Lessons
- Writing a Tiered Lesson

Day 2

- Sharing of products, successes and problems in trying differentiation strategies
- Differentiation for special groups of students (gifted, ELL, special ed, AP and Pre-AP): Needs and strategies
- *Teaching Tools*: Learning modalities, multiple intelligences and learning styles
- Introduction to the Individual Lesson Plan (ILP) format
- Differentiation using learning styles, modalities and multiple intelligences
- Writing an ILP unit

Day 3

- Sharing of products, successes and problems in trying differentiation strategies
- Assessment: What is it and why do we do it?
- Using standards in a differentiated classroom
- Assessing differentiated products and performances
- Developing assessment criteria
- Writing rubrics

Day 4

- Sharing of products, successes and problems in trying differentiation strategies
- Mini-rubrics, checklists and criteria cards
- Tic-Tac-Toe format
- Tic-Tac-Toe assessment
- Grading in a differentiated classroom: Issues and strategies

This workshop series is based on three books by Carolyn Coil:
- *Activities and Assessments for the Differentiated Classroom* – Pieces of Learning
- *Teaching Tools for the 21st Century* – Pieces of Learning
- *Solving the Assessment Puzzle* – Pieces of Learning

Differentiation Training – Sample Three-Year Plan

This is a sample plan of presentations and follow-up activities. The in-house training can be done in Professional Learning Communities. This plan covers three school years.

Session 1 – Year 1 (Outside Consultant)

➢ "Introduction of Differentiation"
➢ Attended by a group of interested and motivated teachers

Session 2 – Year 1 (In-house training)

➢ Follow-up and sharing of differentiation strategies that were tried
➢ *Teaching Tools* book discussion: Curriculum Compacting pgs. 170-171
➢ Discussion of Resident Expert strategy – *Teaching Tools* pg. 177
➢ Work time and final sharing

Session 3 – Year 1 (In-house training)

➢ Follow-up and sharing about using resident experts and curriculum compacting
➢ *Teaching Tools* book discussion: Differentiating for Gifted Students – pgs. 162-164, 169
➢ Discussion of Flexible Grouping strategy – *Teaching Tools* pgs. 175-176
➢ Work time and final sharing

Session 4 – Year 1 (Outside Consultant)

➢ "Differentiation with Multiple Intelligences, Learning Styles and Learning Modalities using the ILP"
➢ Discussion and sharing from previous sessions
➢ Train-the-Trainer for In-house trainers

Session 5 – Year 1 (In-house training)

➢ Follow-up and sharing about use of strategies in individual classrooms
➢ *Teaching Tools* book discussion: Learning Styles – pgs. 29-40
➢ Discussion of Learning Contracts strategy – Teaching Tools pgs. 172-174
➢ Work time and final sharing

Note: During Year 1, teachers who are implementing differentiation strategies in their classrooms will invite other teachers to observe. From this, a new group of interested teachers is formed.

Session 1 Beginning – Year 2 (Outside Consultant)

➤ "Introduction to Differentiation"
➤ Combines information from both outside consultant sessions from Year 1
➤ Attended by a new group of interested teachers. These teachers then join the original group for subsequent trainings.

Session 1 Advanced – Year 2 (Outside Consultant)

➤ "Differentiation using Tiered Lessons and Bloom's Taxonomy"
➤ Discussion and sharing from previous sessions
➤ Train-the-Trainer for In-house trainers

Session 2 – Year 2 (In-house training)

➤ Follow-up and sharing about use of strategies used in classrooms
➤ *Teaching Tools* book discussion: Learning Modalities – pgs. 41-55
➤ Discussion of Individual Lesson Plans (ILP™) – *Teaching Tools* pgs. 16-28
➤ Work time and final sharing

Session 3 – Year 2 (In-house training)

➤ Follow-up and sharing about use of all strategies introduced so far
➤ *Teaching Tools* book discussion: Bloom's Taxonomy – pgs. 56-66, and Tiered Lessons 177-183
➤ Work time to plan lessons, ILPs™ or units with help from in-house trainers

Session 4 – Year 2 (In-house training)

➤ Follow-up and sharing about use of all strategies introduced so far
➤ Teaching Tools book discussion: Multiple Intelligences – pgs. 67-86
➤ Strategy introduced: Using Technology – *Teaching Tools* pgs. 218-229
➤ Work time and sharing

Session 5 – Year 2 (Outside Consultant)

➤ "Assessment Strategies for the Differentiated Classroom"
➤ New books introduced: *Solving the Assessment Puzzle and Activities* and *Assessments for the Differentiated Classroom*

Note: Classroom visitations continue throughout Year 2. Other interested teachers are invited to attend the In-house training sessions. To give them initial training and incorporate them fully, the outside consultant could come and work with them or they could attend a regional or national conference on differentiation.

Session 1 – Year 3 (In-house training)

➢ Follow-up and sharing about use of strategies used in classrooms
➢ *Solving the Assessment Puzzle* book discussion: Assessment terminology – pgs 1-19
➢ Discussion of Standards – *Solving the Assessment Puzzle* pgs. 20-31
➢ Work time and final sharing

Session 2 – Year 3 (In-house training)

➢ Follow-up and sharing about use of all strategies introduced so far
➢ *Solving the Assessment Puzzle* book discussion: Traditional Assessment/Alternative Assessment – pgs. 45-58
➢ Work time to plan lessons, units or work on assessments with help from in-house trainers

Session 3 – Year 3 (Outside Consultant)

➢ "Using Rubrics, Mini-Rubrics and Criteria Cards"
➢ Discussion and sharing from previous sessions
➢ Train-the-Trainer for In-house trainers

Session 4 – Year 3 (In-house training)

➢ Follow-up and sharing about use of all strategies introduced so far
➢ *Solving the Assessment Puzzle* book discussion: About Rubrics – pgs. 91-109
➢ Strategy introduced: Writing Rubrics – *Solving the Assessment Puzzle* pgs. 91-109
➢ Work time and sharing

Session 5 – Year 3 (In-house training)

➢ Follow-up and sharing about use of all strategies introduced so far
➢ *Activities and Assessments for the Differentiated Classroom* book discussion: pgs 11-23
➢ Strategy discussed: Writing Mini-Rubrics and Criteria Cards – *Activities and Assessments for the Differentiated Classroom*
➢ Work time and sharing

This three-year workshop series is based on three books by Carolyn Coil:

• *Activities and Assessments for the Differentiated Classroom* – Pieces of Learning
• *Teaching Tools for the 21st Century* – Pieces of Learning
• *Solving the Assessment Puzzle* – Pieces of Learning

**Traits of a Good Administrator
to Support and Lead Schoolwide Differentiation**

1. Has been trained in and is knowledgeable about differentiation.

2. Has a focus and a goal for the school or district that includes and supports differentiation.

3. Sticks to the goal or vision over a long period of time – doesn't continually jump from one 'new thing' to another.

4. Finds ways to give teachers time to work on units and explore resources.

5. Creative in looking for various sources of funding (such as grants) to pay for training, materials and release time.

6. Shares ideas about what works with other administrators.

7. Willing to open school and classrooms for others to observe.

Potential administrators in your school or district:

_____

_____

_____

Traits of a Good Outside Consultant to Work with Your School

1. Knowledgeable on current educational issues, especially differentiation.

2. Can identify with teachers – teacher friendly.

3. Is inspirational and a motivator with a sense of humor.

4. Knows differentiation strategies and can convey them in a practical way so teachers can use them.

5. Has fresh ('cutting edge') ideas, yet knows how to start at the beginning with teachers who have no training in differentiation.

6. Can give appropriate feedback to teacher questions as they arise

7. Can come on a regular basis – not "once down, done".

8. Willing to answer questions via phone or email in between district or school visits.

9. Is affordable within your school, district or professional development budget.

Potential consultants:

_____

_____

_____

Traits of Good In-House Resident Experts
Supporting Schoolwide Differentiation

1. Implement differentiation in their own classrooms.

2. Show positive results of using differentiation including gains in test scores.

3. Knowledgeable of philosophy and strategies used in differentiation.

4. Able to answer questions from colleagues.

5. Can motivate other teachers.

6. Are organized and can plan training.

7. Are personable and are good listeners.

8. Are not judgmental and are supportive of new ideas.

9. Willing to have other teachers visit their classrooms.

Potential teachers in your school or district:

_____

_____

_____

Plan for Schoolwide Differentiation

I. Teachers to involve:

II. Initial training and motivation:

III. Training Sessions (How Many?) Topics for each:

IV. In-house follow-up sessions and sharing:

V. Time for planning and writing differentiated lessons/units:

VI. Resources needed:

Developing a Demonstration Classroom Program

1. Make a list of differentiation strategies that are being used in classrooms in your school or district.

2. Decide how many teachers you would like to have as Demonstration Classroom Teachers.

3. Meet with principals and other administrators to explain the program and ask them to nominate teachers to be Demonstration Classroom Teachers.

4. Contact the nominated teachers to find out if they would be interested in being Demonstration Classroom Teachers.

5. Develop an Information Form to be given to each teacher or use the one on the next page. You may need to change the list of strategies to reflect what teachers are doing in your school or district.

6. Schedule a Demonstration Classroom Teacher Training session. During the training session, discuss each of the differentiation strategies listed and ask each teacher to fill out the Information Form. Each teacher should check no more than four strategies. Try to get a wide range of different strategies represented in the Demonstration Classroom Program.

7. During the training session, have each Demonstration Classroom Teacher write up how specific differentiation strategies are implemented in his/her classroom.

8. Publish a Demonstration Classroom Handbook and/or put the information on the school or district website. Include all of the Information Forms and a brief definition of each strategy. Also include an application form for visiting a Demonstration Classroom.

9. Schedule Visiting Teachers as they apply to visit a Demonstration Classroom. Coordinate dates with the Demonstration Teacher. Before the visit, send a packet of information including the Demonstration Teacher's strategy write-up and any other reading you want the Visiting Teacher to complete before the visit.

10. After each visit, collect evaluation forms from both the Demonstration Teacher and the Visiting Teacher.

11. Plan an event at the end of the school year to honor and thank the Demonstration Classroom Teachers.

Demonstration Teacher Information Form

Name _____

School _____

Grade level/Subject_____

Phone _____ E-mail _____

Differentiation Strategies demonstrated:

_____ Flexible Grouping   _____ Learning Contracts

_____ Curriculum Compacting   _____ ILP

_____ Resident Experts   _____ Tic-Tac-Toe

_____ Learning Centers   _____ Technology

_____ Tiered Instruction   _____ Literature Circles

_____ Use of Learning Profiles   _____ Independent Study

_____ Pre-assessment   _____ Formative Assessment

_____ Anchoring Activities   _____ Questivities™

General information about your school:

General information about your classroom:

General information about your students:

General information about you:

Nuts and Bolts Issues

In order for teachers to differentiate curriculum well, the learning environment (classrooms, storerooms, workrooms and/or office areas) should have:

➢ A comprehensive store of resources for both large group instruction and small group or individual activities. Resources include reference and supplemental materials for students at all levels. Teachers who don't have such a store are severely limited in their ability to provide creative, engaging, hands-on, differentiated lessons. The best teachers seem to have the most stuff. They need it and use it.

➢ A place to plan, create, and inventory materials used in classrooms

➢ A place to store student work in various stages of completion. Teachers who can't do this can't assign projects whose product is larger than a spiral notebook. Problems occur when two teachers share the same room. Both store student work and other materials and the room takes on the aspect of a fire marshal's nightmare.

Teachers need to:

➢ Use the physical classroom itself to enhance instruction. Good teachers use their walls, boards, ceilings, doors, and windows to post important information, display student work, reinforce fundamental knowledge, celebrate student accomplishments, post the class rules, and in general create an inviting and stimulating learning environment.

➢ Have a way to set up and take down activities in the room before and after class. This is required for doing hands-on, project based work.

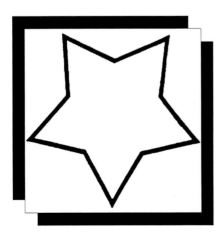

How Parents Can Help
With Differentiated Curriculum

1. Understand that all students in the same class will not always have exactly the same assignment. Assignments for gifted students may be more challenging and more difficult. Assignments for special education students or English Language Learners may be shorter or modified in other ways.

2. Encourage learning and help your child understand that learning is the main goal of school, not grades or points or competing against others.

3. Be supportive and interested in what your child is learning, but do not do your child's homework for him or her. If he or she has a major project to do, find out ahead of time how much parental help is acceptable. There is a delicate balance between too much parental assistance and not enough.

4. Know what is being studied in school and share any resources you may have about this topic. Informal conversations are always helpful and usually increase your child's interest in and connections to the topic.

5. Whenever possible, point out the relationships between what is being learned at school and things that are going on in other parts of your child's life. Links to your family's history, culture or experiences are also valuable.

6. Help your child with organizational and study skills. These are not automatic for most students!

7. Understand that the learning process (learning how to learn) is just as important as learning basic skills and knowledge. Parents can often help with skills and knowledge-based tasks, but you should allow your child to discover some of the process skills himself.

8. Help your child discover special areas of interest for in-depth study. Model the learning process by being excited about learning yourself!

9. Know the terminology and strategies used in differentiation. Some words to understand include learning contracts, curriculum compacting, flexible grouping, student choice activities, Individual Lesson Plan, Tic-Tac-Toe, rubrics, and independent study. (Add your own words to this list)

10. Inquire about how grading is being done in your child's differentiated classroom. It is important that you understand the meaning behind the grade.

To Summarize . . .
Keys to Successful Schoolwide
or Districtwide Differentiation

➤ Successful schoolwide or districtwide differentiation doesn't happen overnight. It is a long process that takes time, effort, planning, practice, ongoing teacher training and a wealth of practical strategies that teachers can implement effectively.

➤ There are fourteen general guidelines that will help you as you make a plan to put differentiation into practice in your school or district.

➤ Successful schoolwide or districtwide differentiation comes as a result of planned professional development activities along with follow-up and practice in the classroom.

➤ It is important to look for administrators, an outside consultant and some in-house experts to take the leadership in bringing differentiation to your school or district.

➤ Demonstration Classrooms featuring teachers using differentiation strategies are a wonderful way to show other teachers how differentiation actually works.

➤ For differentiation to be implemented in a school, the learning environment must include storage areas, places for materials, and lots of classroom and wall space that can be used to enhance learning.

➤ Parents need to be informed about how a differentiated classroom works and what their role should be in encouraging and helping their child.

Index

Professional Staff Development with Carolyn Coil

from Pieces of Learning

Carolyn is an internationally known speaker, author, trainer, consultant and educator. In her workshops, professional development courses, seminars and keynotes, she is an enthusiastic, motivating and energetic presenter. Carolyn works with teachers, parents and students offering practical strategies for raising student achievement, differentiating curriculum, implementing a variety of assessment strategies, and dealing with the problems and challenges associated with preparing ourselves and our children for living and working in the 21st Century.

Carolyn presents a variety of stimulating and practical workshops. She is well regarded in the educational community both nationally and internationally. Carolyn custom designs keynotes, workshops and other training activities based on your specific needs and your requests.

In addition to providing training in individual schools and school districts, Carolyn is a frequent presenter at regional workshops and state or national conferences.

Expertise in

- ➢ Differentiating Curriculum and Instruction
- ➢ Assessment Strategies
- ➢ Motivating Underachievers
- ➢ Gifted Education
- ➢ Learning Styles/Modalities/Multiple Intelligences

Types of Training Provided

- ➢ Sustained long-term professional development
- ➢ Keynotes
- ➢ Full day teacher workshops
- ➢ Small group sessions
- ➢ Train-the-Trainer
- ➢ Developing curriculum with teachers

Staff Development Resource Bundles

Pieces of Learning offers Workshop Bundles
Speaker fee and multiple-copies of books (at a discounted price).
Train-the-Trainer Staff Development with PowerPoint and Book Bundles.

Call *Pieces of Learning* to schedule staff development
and order quantities of books/resources at a discount.
1-800-729-5137   www.piecesoflearning.com

More Resources from Carolyn Coil

available from *Pieces of Learning*
1-800-729-5137

www.piecesoflearning.com
www.differentiatedresources.com
www.creativelearningconsultants.com